W9-BHB-434

• THE BOOK OF •
HARD CHOICES

**ALSO BY
JAMES A. AUTRY**

---

*The Spirit of Retirement: Creating a Life
of Meaning and Personal Growth*

*The Servant Leader: How to Build a Creative Team, Develop
Great Morale, and Improve Bottom-Line Performance*

Love and Profit: The Art of Caring Leadership

Life and Work: A Manager's Search for Meaning

Confessions of an Accidental Businessman

*Real Power: Business Lessons from the Tao Te Ching
(with Stephen Mitchell)*

Nights Under a Tin Roof

Life After Mississippi

• THE BOOK OF •
HARD CHOICES

HOW TO MAKE THE RIGHT DECISIONS AT
WORK AND KEEP YOUR SELF-RESPECT

JAMES A. AUTRY

AND PETER ROY

Morgan Road Books
New York

MORGAN ROAD BOOKS

Published by Morgan Road Books

Copyright © 2006 by James A. Autry and Peter Roy

All Rights Reserved

Published in the United States by Morgan Road Books, an
imprint of The Doubleday Broadway Publishing Group, a
division of Random House, Inc., New York.
www. morganroadbooks.com

MORGAN ROAD BOOKS and the M colophon are trademarks
of Random House, Inc.

Book design by Michael Collica

Library of Congress Cataloging-in-Publication Data

Autry, James A.
    The book of hard choices : how to make the right
decisions at work and keep your self-respect / by James A.
Autry and Peter Roy. — 1st ed.
        p. cm.
    Includes index.
    1. Decision making. I. Roy, Peter, 1956– II. Title.

HD30.23.A98 2006
658.4'03—dc22
                                                        2006046465

ISBN-13: 978-0-7679-2258-6
ISBN-10: 0-7679-2258-1

PRINTED IN THE UNITED STATES OF AMERICA

10 9 8 7 6 5 4 3 2 1

First Edition

Dozens of executives in various fields agreed to have their stories told in this book. All these stories are true, but in some cases, at the request of our interviewees, the names of people, organizations, and some accompanying details have been changed to prevent possible embarrassment. We've noted in each chapter which names are real and which names have been changed.

To Sally, who knows what hard choices are, and makes them with courage and commitment.

—James A. Autry

In memory of my father, William Alexander Roy, a man of great integrity who taught me the importance of "always doing what you say you're going to do."

And to my daughters, Emma and Molly, who have taught me so much about making hard choices. My love and thanks.

—Peter Roy

CONTENTS

In researching and preparing to write this book, the authors had numerous conversations with friends and business associates. Then we interviewed and heard the stories of more than thirty leaders, and from those selected the stories published here.

All these conversations and interviews contributed in one way or another to this book. Thus, we thank Lex Alexander, Lynn Baker, Chip Baird, Cathy Black, Howard Behar, Patricia DeJong, Steve Demos, Ken Dychtwald, Betty Sue Flowers, John Gans, Michael Gartner, Tom Gould, Doug Greene, Barry Griswold, Matt Handbury, Jack Herschend, Gary Hirshberg, Alan Houghton, Ron R. Ingle, Matthew Jenkins, Dr. Robert Khayat, Doug Lehrman, Elizabeth Lesser, Leslie Lundgren, Mary Middleton, Doris Mitchell, Hal Northrop, Dr. Will Norton, George Pierson, Gil Pritchard, Charles Purves, Drake Sadler, Tom Sawner, Bobbi Schlesinger, David Stein, Daniel Thomas, Dwight Tierney, Tim Tuff, John Young, and Governor Tom Vilsack.

Plus a special thanks to John Elstrott and Walter Robb.

We also acknowledge the yeoman service of Theresa

Graziano, our transcriber, who spent hour upon hour listening to tapes and deciphering words from the wide variety of accents, including Australian, English, New England, and Southern. Thank you, Theresa; we could not have done it without you.

And we appreciate the dedication and hard work of our agent, the ever-ebullient Doris Michaels, and her staff.

Finally, our love and appreciation for the two people who had to keep smiling while we struggled and kvetched and cursed our way through the process: our wives, Sally Pederson and Gillian Roy.

• THE BOOK OF •
HARD CHOICES

THE ASPECTS OF INTEGRITY

It's more about who you are than what you do.

INTEGRITY IS ONE of those words that rolls easily off the tongue. Like love. Or trust. Or morality. Or ethics. Those words all have one characteristic in common: They don't mean a thing until they become behavior. Before then, they're just words representing a feeling or an intention, nothing more.

You can say "I love you" or "I trust you" until the end of time, but until you behave with love or trust, everyone will be better off if you just say nothing.

Integrity is no different. It's easy to talk about and even easy to feel and to demonstrate, as long as everything is going well and nothing comes along to put your integrity to the test. In other words, your sense of integrity, while admirable, is not made fully real until you have to live it in difficult and challenging circumstances.

Perhaps you think your integrity will not be put to the test. You could be right, but not likely. The authors have spent, cumulatively, almost sixty years in corporate life, plus another eighteen years as consultants, and we have yet to see a manager or leader who has not faced pressures and temptations that threaten to derail the best of intentions.

One of the major misunderstandings about the choices you'll face is the belief that the really tough ones will be about money. Not true. The choices that will create the most frustration and anxiety, as well as the greatest challenge to your ability to maintain an ethical balance, will be about relationships, not about money. In the scheme of things, money is easy; relationships are hard.

And don't think those pressures will be only about the big issues so often associated with leadership positions. To the contrary, the challenges come along every day and may seem on the surface to be insignificant, so you have to stay alert because the "little" daily choices are every bit as important, and do as much to shape and to demonstrate your integrity, as the big dilemmas.

Once you recognize that your integrity is on the line every day, then your work life takes on a different meaning. You realize that as you begin to face the choices and make the ones that reflect your true self, then you can have an enormous impact on your workplace, regardless of your position in the organizational hierarchy.

For instance, consider this common situation: Bosses should never criticize one employee to another employee, but they do it, and you may find yourself pulled into a conversation like that one day. Perhaps the boss is trying honestly to get your opinion of the other person, perhaps trying to dig for information, perhaps looking for affirmation of his or her already-held opinion, or perhaps just blowing off frustrations.

The tempting choice is to offer a hearty agreement and hope the boss sees your brilliance. But that could be risky. The easy choice is to nod and be noncommittal, seeming to agree without really saying anything. Then comes the hard choice: not so much to argue with the boss as to honestly express your feeling that you're not comfortable in this situation. Yes, this can also be risky, and it will take courage.

What about other kinds of negative talk? There's gossip and loose talk at almost every level in every organization. When it begins, do you join right in or do you refuse to participate? When someone makes a snide remark about a fellow worker or colleague, do you let it slide and walk away, thus implying that you agree with the comment or that you don't have an opinion? Or do you actively condemn that kind of negative discourse? Listen, it's easier to walk away; it's difficult to say, "I really think it's counterproductive to talk about people that way."

You may respond, "I can't defend everyone who's being talked about." Of course not, but if you do it even once or twice you will make the point dramatically enough that the gossip will stop—at least around you. And that in itself will have an impact on others, perhaps giving them the courage to follow your example.

Gossip leads to bullying. It's an old story: If somehow we can define someone else as not worthy, as a lesser person or worker, as someone not to be respected, the next step is to ostracize that person. This leads to a bullying mentality toward the person, who then suffers psychological if not physical damage.

As organizations have pressured their workers to work harder and work longer, they have helped create an atmosphere in which the concepts of civility and cooperation are lost in the hurry-scurry of a high-pressure workplace.

This means you have to be careful with your own language. You must take time to express yourself calmly and carefully, especially when telling people something they may not like to hear. There's a thin line between being frank or honest and being tactless. There's also a measure of integrity in how you speak to people, in your body language, in your tone of voice.

The authors visited with one manager who seemed universally thought of as arrogant and overbearing. When asked about this perception, he replied, "I'm just being honest. If people can't take honesty, tough." This manager didn't know the difference between honesty and bluntness; thus, he regularly undermined the importance of his message by the aggressive way he delivered it. This then became an issue of integrity when the manager disregarded the feelings of others and, rather than examining his own behavior, blamed his fellow workers for not being able to "take the truth when they hear it."

The authors have visited many workplaces in which all the talk about "team effort" is just that: talk.

There are a thousand acts of duplicity and dishonesty every day, some large and some small, some of which undoubtedly take place in your organization. What about even the so-called "trivial stuff," like stretching the old expense report, doing personal work on the organization's time and equipment, or appropriating supplies for oneself? Everybody does it, right? And those people in the executive suite get all kinds of perks, so it's only fair that everybody deserves a little of the action, right?

The question for all of us is, "Are we going to resist or just play along the path of least resistance?" Admittedly, resisting the status quo is difficult, but acquiescing to the daily injustices and dishonesties will take its toll on your very spirit.

The Tao-te-ching says that the journey of a thousand miles

begins with a single step, so a full life of integrity depends on individual acts of courage in living your values every day.

The need to demonstrate this courage just seems to be part of life, and especially of organizational life. The problem is that integrity is a personal matter, and within any organization, it is the people who create the environment of integrity.

To be sure, there are, in any organization, emphases on two aspects of operational behavior: ethicality and legality. What's ethical and what's legal? You can find several kinds of organizational resources and guidelines in these areas, and almost every business of any size has a statement of ethics—but so what? Unless the people, in their own sense of integrity, behave ethically in the organization, the statement of ethics is just that: a statement. In fact, you can bet that every one of the now-infamous corporations—Enron, Tyco, World-Com, and others—had perfectly fine statements of ethics, well reasoned and well written, published in employee publications and the annual report, posted on bulletin boards, and so on.

So what happened? Simple. Ethical behavior depends not on policies and guidelines and high-sounding polysyllabic statements, but on individual integrity.

There are plenty of instances in which what is legal may very well not be ethical; thus, an emphasis on what's legal can get many managers in trouble: "If it's legal, it must be okay." This has often become a very convenient hiding place for people who don't want to use their own integrity to evaluate the ethics of what they're doing or have done, only the legality.

The reasons for this are obvious enough. We are a nation of laws, we bind virtually every agreement with a contract, we dictate that behavior must be legal.

But ethicality is not about contracts, it's about covenants. Contracts are written with all sorts of provisions for reparation, damage assessments, and other legal repercussions. On the other hand, covenants are moral understandings and are "enforceable" only by the moral intention of the participants, by their commitment to do what they say they are going to do.

While ethics is an institutional term, the living of an ethical work and management life nonetheless depends absolutely on the moral compasses of the people who must make ethics real by the way they choose to behave.

This is where integrity comes in.

Integrity itself is never institutional, it is always personal. Just as there is no such thing as "business ethics," only "people ethics," there is no such thing as a "corporation of integrity." If a business has such a reputation, it is only because its people live with integrity and exhibit it in all their relationships.

The challenge, of course, is that the values of integrity and morality in organizational life, such as in a business, rarely come packaged in easy-to-apply actions. More often than not, the hard choices that people face in organizational life, particularly those in management and leadership positions, reside somewhere in the gray areas of moral judgment. So the first hard choice a person of integrity must make is to choose to live, both personally and professionally, in a way that embodies the aspects of integrity.

THE ASPECTS OF INTEGRITY

Integrity can be defined in many ways and in ever-increasing levels of complexity, but in researching this book, the authors identified five aspects of integrity that seem most important:

1. Doing what you say you're going to do;
2. Putting other people's needs first;
3. Behaving courageously;
4. Ensuring the common good above all; and
5. Maintaining your focus on respect, honesty, trust, and fairness.

Once again, these are words that roll easily off the tongue and mean nothing unless they translate into behavior. If you are in a leadership position, you must understand that, like it or not, you set the moral and ethical tone for your organization, be it a multinational corporation or a department of three people within a larger organization. You should live these aspects of integrity personally and also make every effort for them to become organizational or institutional behavior.

The authors don't claim to be perfect in how we've lived our professional lives. We made mistakes like everyone else, but somehow we also managed to get to a point that our leadership practices, for the most part (we still don't claim to be perfect), became consonant with our values and our sense of integrity.

We recall many examples, but in order to make the point that we've been there and made the hard choices, you will find two stories from our own experience in chapter 23.

We are not saying that we or the other people in this book always made the right choices. In fact, you may not agree with some of the choices they made. And sometimes even the right choice turns out badly, as in the case of Daniel Thomas (page 121), but their choices are always thoughtful and always made from an attitude of integrity.

To gather the stories in this book, we talked with dozens of executives in various fields, including not only business but also the military, public service, and education. All these stories are true, but in some cases, at the request of our interviewee, the names of people and organizations have been changed to prevent possible embarrassment. This in no way diminishes the lessons they teach or their impact.

We believe that the power of this book comes from the real-life, in-the-workplace experiences that these executives have been so generously willing to share. None had easy choices, but that's the point: Integrity is not about easy choices, it's about the courage to make the right choices. And those are the hard choices.

LOOK THE OTHER WAY OR FACE DOWN THE CORRUPTION?

Is it true that nice guys always finish last?

IN 1972, DAVID STEIN was enjoying a terrific career on the East Coast with the largest home-building company in the world. He was so successful at it, in fact, that he wasn't sure whether he was good or just lucky, so he decided to move to California.

"I liked the company I was with," David explains, "but frankly, it was the largest home builder in the world because it built houses the way Ford builds cars, mass-produced. I wanted to do something more creative. I chose California because it was, and probably still is, the leader in terms of planned community development and architectural and interior design."

He went to work as a project manager for ACDI, one of the largest planned community developers in the country. Probably the company's most important development was in Laguna Beach, a seven-thousand-acre planned community that stretched from the Pacific Ocean to the interstate highway that connects Los Angeles and San Diego. The prospect of working in this area seemed like a dream job for David, but he quickly realized that all was not well.

"Not only was the company not run the way my former company was," he recalls, "but I felt there was real corruption within the company and it was very disheartening for me."

David's concerns had to do with the process of getting projects approved. "It was clear that in order to get a project approved, it required political support, so the company's over-riding concern was getting the support of politicians and not of the community."

David wanted to manage good projects, but he found that at this company it was less important to manage good projects and more important to manage projects that could get political approval. "The way to do that was support the campaigns of politicians. And what made this corrupt in my opinion was that the decisions were not to be made on the basis of the projects' merit but purely on political influence."

David made another uncomfortable discovery. ACDI had a terrible reputation in the community itself. "They used to say that ACDI is a four-letter word," he laughs. "It was clear to me that my first priority as a project manager was to build bridges with the community."

David felt, not only as a matter of personal principle but also in the interest of the business, that a company should strive to be a good citizen of the communities in which it operates, and he personally intended to be a good citizen of the community. He could not choose to compromise either his personal or his business principles.

He knew, however, that building bridges was not going to be easy. Before David arrived, the California legislature responded to concerns about development by passing the California Coastal Act, which established the California Coastal Commission to set up criteria for development.

David explains ACDI's response as the reason for community hostility toward the company: "ACDI had a huge property on the coast, so to beat the clock before the new law took effect, they started grading the property. They moved millions of yards of earth, and they did it in twenty-hour shifts, bringing in big spotlights so they could work night and day. There was also a piece of property on the sea that was a very popular surf spot. They cut off public access to it. They just seemed to do pretty much everything they could to piss off the people in the community.

"Even though I worked for the company, I came to feel that the bad reputation was deserved and that I should try to do something about it."

His bosses did not think it was necessary. The system was working for them because of the political influence they had garnered. Here's the process: First the project managers of the various companies presented their projects to a planning commission. Often, representatives of the community would oppose the projects before the commission. If the projects were then not approved by the commission, the companies were allowed to appeal this decision to the county board of supervisors, and, of course, if the companies had made the appropriate campaign contributions, they always won the appeal.

"But," David says, "there was more and more community resentment being built through these practices. It could not continue, and besides, I felt it was utterly corrupt to game the system in this way."

David began his own initiatives, meeting with community

leaders and laying out his plans. They were suspicious. "First, I was with ACDI, which was bad enough, but there was also my own personal image problem. I came to one of the most conservative counties in the country, Orange County, with a George McGovern sticker on my car; I had long hair and a Fu Manchu mustache. The people I met with either had a flattop or a buzz cut. To say they were skeptical and suspicious is an understatement. But as I got to know them and convince them that I had the best interests of the community at heart, they put up with me.

"I had a lot of problems because my bosses thought I was an idiot. They said, 'This is not the way it's done.' I said yes it is, and eventually this is what will be our survival because the time will come when we're going to have a lot of problems getting projects approved."

At about the same time that David was reaching out to the community, a wealthy construction company owner, Ralph Dietrick, decided to run for the county board of supervisors. He invested a lot of his money in the campaign to unseat a longtime supervisor and was elected. He quickly moved to establish his power by donating money to other supervisors' campaigns and helping them get elected, the result of which was that Dietrick could always produce three votes, a majority, of the supervisors on any issue.

"He became famous," David says, "for asking, 'Do you know how to count to three?' "

During this time, David was not sure he would be able to remain with the company. But he did not want to give up on his goal of getting the community support that would convince the planning commission to approve the projects without having to appeal to a corrupt supervisor and his cronies.

He almost lost his job when he accompanied his boss to a

meeting with Dietrick, a meeting that in David's view was not necessary.

"I was working on a project," David recalls, "where there was a property line that went straight through some hilltops, and really it didn't make any sense. It was an artificial line. We needed a road to the top of a hill, but putting the road on one side or the other of the property line would mean destroying the hilltops and doing tremendous grading damage. So I had worked out an agreement with the neighbor that we would trade some land back and forth because it really wasn't buildable land anyway. This way we could snake the road through and not do environmental damage. The deal was a bit complicated and I was proud of having pulled it off."

But David's boss, the general manager, was not happy. "You can't do that," he said. When David asked why, the boss said, "That son of a bitch [the neighbor] screwed me ten years ago and I'm not doing anything that might help him."

David was stunned. "But we can't do the road the other way," he said. "It will cost a lot of extra money and besides, it's wrong."

The boss made him change the road.

"I thought about quitting then and there," David says, "but it wasn't the most important thing in a very big project and while it aggravated me, I thought the overall project was more important than that one issue."

David dutifully took the project to the planning commission, and of course it was not approved because of the road. Then came the appeal to the board of supervisors. David's boss insisted that David accompany him to a private meeting with Dietrick, who by that time had become chairman of the board of supervisors.

"My boss wanted me to go because he needed me to explain the issue because he didn't fully understand it. All he knew is that he didn't want his old enemy to get the road worked out.

"Well, I bristled against it but I went to the meeting, where I sat silently somewhat like a petulant child. It was clear to everyone that I didn't want to be there."

This was to be the first time David got to witness the corruption firsthand. When his boss, Don, began to explain the situation, he stopped and said that David would explain it.

"So I told them the truth," David says. "I told them that the plan was justifiably appealed because the road should not go where Don wants it to go."

His boss shouted at David, "That's not the issue," then turning to Dietrick, said, "I want that road there and that's it. I don't want to help this guy."

Then Dietrick turned to one of his aides and a lobbyist who was in the room and asked, "Has Don bought a table to my dinner party?"

Don said proudly, "Yes, I did."

"Understand that this was a $1,200 table," David says, "which is probably equivalent to $10,000 in today's dollars. So I just kept my mouth shut."

Then Dietrick looked at Don and at the lobbyist and said, "Boys, this looks like a two-table problem to me."

At this point, David got up and left the meeting without saying anything. In the car with Don, he asked, "How could you do that? I did what you wanted me to do."

"Yes," said Don, "and you didn't do it right."

David responded, "No, Don, you're wrong. I did do it right and damned if I was going to sit there while you negotiated the number of tables you were going to buy to get his vote. Excuse me, his three votes."

David continued his work with the community leaders even though Don thought it unnecessary. "But I was being successful, really, and I know Don liked me, he just didn't understand. He was doing it the way everyone always had done it."

David was determined to change the company and end the corruption. The turning point came when he developed and presented to the planning commission the first project that did not have to be appealed to the board of supervisors.

"There was a very feisty planning commissioner nicknamed 'Gravel Gertie,' " David recalls, "and the people in the community loved her because she was fighting the development. I remember the first time I had to come up before her. She hated me without knowing me because I was ACDI. She wouldn't meet with me before the hearing because she thought that I would try to put pressure on her.

"On the day of the hearing I had the support of the community for my project, and I was sandwiched in between two other developers who had unpopular projects. The planning commission room was packed and there were people waiting outside.

"The first developer presented his case, and then the community went on and on about how terrible the plan was. This took so much time, the commission had to delay the decision for two weeks. So when everybody came back after that, they were angry.

"After the first group left, I was up. The county staff made their presentation and recommended approval of my project. Then the chairwoman, Gravel Gertie, growled, 'Now we're going to hear from the applicant.' "

David had decided that he would try to lighten up the proceedings with humor. This is not always a good idea because it can seem as if you are not taking the situation seriously, but David felt it was worth the risk.

"I hoped not to sound like an arrogant smart aleck," he says. "But when the chairwoman said, 'Now we're going to hear from the applicant,' I stepped to the podium and said, 'Well, my name is David Stein, but actually if it's okay, I'd like to say I'm the builder because if you say I'm the applicant, it will be really kind of disappointing for my mother. She thinks I'm a builder. I've been telling her I'm a builder, and if she finds out I'm only an applicant, it'll be a problem.'

"The room broke into laughter, but the chairwoman turned red. I mean, she was really angry. But it broke the tension in the room. She slammed her gavel down two or three times and said, 'Mr. Stein, please continue.' And I said, 'Okay, I work for ACDI.' Then I said, 'Could I amend that?' She looked at me like I was crazy. And I said, actually instead of builder, would it be okay if I said I was a doctor because my mother really thinks I'm a doctor."

Again, everyone in the room laughed, and David wondered if he had gone too far or if he had indeed undercut some of the tension and hostility.

Then he changed the tone. "Look," he said, "I'm very proud of this project and I think it's something that's groundbreaking. The staff has supported it and I think the community, probably to your surprise, is here to support this project, not to protest against it, so I'll give up the rest of my time and just respond to questions."

Then the community leaders, one by one, stood to support the project. Afterward, the chairwoman called David back to the podium. "Mr. Stein, oh sorry, I mean Doctor Stein, I want to compliment you. The project is quite amazing, especially coming from ACDI."

After this success, David began a relationship with the chairwoman that led to a collaboration between the two of them in a program called "Tin Cup" (Time is now to clean up politics).

The timing was perfect for David because the company's business had slowed, and his boss, Don, was fired. David was named general manager of the division.

And this is where the real story of hard choices begins. The first thing David did was fire the lobbyist. Then he announced that the company would no longer give any political contribution to any politician except for the one supervisor from the company's own district, and only then if it seemed justified. This was in addition to his Tin Cup activities, through which he and the Orange County Homebuilders Association were promoting a $1,000 campaign contribution limit.

There was also another home builders group composed of the major builders in the area. David, as general manager of his division, attended those meetings as well. He remembers one at which some of the "icons of the industry," in his words, approached him and said, "David, we have to talk about this thing called Tin Cup because it's completely unfair and we have to block it. So, David, you need to leave the room."

David asked why. "So we can discuss it and we don't want to discuss it in front of you."

Only one builder supported David and said, "You can't make David leave. He's a member of the group."

When they again asked David to leave, he responded, "Gentlemen, if all of you would like to leave and talk separately, you're welcome to it. I'm staying." David was not trying to be obstinate or obstructive, and he was not trying to be the conscience of the group. But he had thought through the situation and felt that all the businesses represented would suffer if they tried to operate outside the concerns of the community rather than with the community. He hoped that his presence would encourage some other members of the group to find the courage to resist a groupthink mentality.

They then continued their discussion in front of David. He was shocked by what he heard. "One of the things they said was that this was undemocratic. I said, 'Beg your pardon?' and they said, 'It's not fair because if you just go by the votes, then the people really have all the say and the only way we can be even is by giving money. It's the only way we can have justice.' I mean, this was their mentality. They thought what I was doing was cheating them out of their inalienable rights."

What David had done, with his own company policy as well as with Tin Cup, sent shock waves through the political establishment.

"I was summoned, and I do mean summoned, to an 8:00 A.M. meeting with Ralph Dietrick. It was quite an experience. In fact, I'd always thought he was tough, brilliant, and effective, and I would have admired him if he wasn't also corrupt. He'd made his fortune as a contractor and now he was the most powerful politician in Orange County and was spreading his tentacles into San Diego. He came to the point. It was quite dramatic.

"He said, 'Look, Stein, I don't care what you do, but you can't do this. You can't fire your lobbyist and you can't stop giving political contributions. I don't care about you. I really don't care about ACDI, but if you get away with this, if I let you get away with this, then you're going to ruin the game, because once people see they don't have to pay, who's going to pay and the whole system breaks down. So here's the deal, I want to be clear. I promise you will never get another project approved as long as you have this policy. Besides that, your parent company has other interests such as an insurance company here. That company does a lot of business with the county. I'll break their contracts. I mean, the president of the insurance company is a friend of mine. We go fishing and play poker together. He'll go to company headquarters, and they're not going to give a goddamn about some kid running the company here when you can't get anything approved. So grow up or you're finished.' "

It was a moment of truth, one of several that were to follow in the next months. David stood his ground. "Look, this is the way it's going to be. I'm not trying to bring down the system and I don't care what you do with the other guys. I'm just doing this my way because, honestly, I don't have another way of doing it. This is not an option."

"So we're going to war," said Dietrick, then smiling, he added something surprising: "Kid, you've got balls. You know something, David, I wish I had a son like you. If I had a son like you, then I could sleep at night because you could run the business while I'm running the county." Then, pausing, he said, "All right, this is your last chance. Where are you on this?"

David responded, "Look, I'm not your son. I'm not going to be your son. But it's a shame because just as you wish I was your son, Supervisor Dietrick, I wish you weren't corrupt. You are absolutely the best supervisor we have in this county. You're the only person who can get things done and who understands all the processes and issues. But you are corrupt. So that means I'm going to war not only against a corrupt politician, but against the best one. I frankly wish you would consider just being a great politician."

Dietrick, still smiling, looked David in the eye and said, "Let the war begin."

This conflict created a great deal of buzz in the building industry and the conventional wisdom was that David would soon be out of a job.

"I wasn't worried about that," says David, "but I was worried about my 470 employees, not a small group. And I had a lot of self-doubt about this battle. Was I just being Don Quixote fighting windmills? I mean, it was one thing for me to fight my battle. I was young. I was single. I was idealistic. I was not just putting my job in jeopardy, but I was putting those 470 people in jeopardy and their spouses and kids and grandparents. I was playing with their lives much more than mine. I felt the weight of those people on my shoulders. This was much more difficult for me than any concern about what Dietrick might do to me.

"Almost every morning my question was, 'Is this an ego trip? Are you so arrogant that you know you're right?' There really wasn't a question in my mind that I was right, but was it the right thing to put these people's jobs in jeopardy? And we'd done wonderful things in the company. These people believed in me and supported me, but when I looked them in the eye I could see the fear, I could hear their questions, 'Why are you doing this?' 'Are you sure?' It was very painful."

What David was going through are the very questions that make hard choices so hard. Rarely will there be a simple black-and-white decision. In this case, David was clearly making the correct choice between right and wrong, but in any organization there are almost no decisions, no choices that don't affect people beyond yourself or your close circle of colleagues. The question then becomes "What's more right?" or "What's more wrong?" If you do the right thing and the company goes out of business and people lose their livelihoods and the community loses that tax base, did the "right thing" really turn out right?

There also are considerations of timing. Can this decision wait or should it be made now? Is there something on the horizon, a change in a law or a change in company management, that might affect the decision? If so, can you live with the present uncomfortable situation until a time when you can be sure your decision will produce the desired result? These were the painful questions and dilemmas David faced throughout this period.

Then came the real battle. "About four or five months after Dietrick declared war on me, I was approached by a young assistant district attorney who said, 'David, I want to bring down Ralph Dietrick. I know he's telling everyone he's going to destroy you. So do you have the courage to testify against him in a grand jury hearing?' When I asked what was involved, he told me not to worry, that I would be brought in secretly and would give secret testimony. He also said that the only way the system was going to be broken was if people had the courage to testify. So I agreed."

On the day of the testimony, David was escorted secretly into the building and entered the hearing room. "So I sit down and find myself facing one of Dietrick's closest card-playing, drinking, and fishing buddies. And I thought, hell, I might just as well dictate a copy of this for Dietrick because it's going straight to him.

"But it didn't really make any difference because I knew he was going to know one way or another that I testified against him. So I testified for a very uncomfortable hour and a half. Then I left. And then all hell broke loose."

David got a call from company headquarters in Greenwich, telling him that one of the top company officers was coming to see him. When the two met, the officer said, "David, you got into something way over your head. We've been told that ACDI will never ever get another project approved unless we fire you. As long as you're here, we're dead. And secondly, we also are not going to get any more insurance contracts for Orange County and are going to lose the contracts we have. This is not even considering the smaller businesses we have. So, you understand we have to fire you."

David's response was not what the officer expected. "Yes, I understand completely," said David, "but what's really a shame is that you can't fire me. The one thing I have not injured here is the reputation of ACDI. Look, for the first time since I've been here, ACDI is a champion of justice instead of being a four-letter word. People think we're trying to make a difference, not just because I'm working with the community but because I testified against Dietrick.

"So your dilemma is that until the grand jury gives its verdict, you can't fire me. If you do, you're admitting that you're corrupt, that you're as corrupt as Dietrick. So if you fire me now, you lose. If, on the other hand, Dietrick does not get indicted, you can fire me."

"But David, he's never going to get indicted," the officer said. "Nobody believes you're going to bring down the most powerful politician in Orange County. The worst thing is that one of his guys will take the fall for him."

David replied that if Dietrick was not indicted, he would resign without protest and would spare the company the bother of firing him.

As the months passed and the tension built, David stayed at his job and tried to support his people in their insecurities about the situation. Then one day, the assistant district attorney called and said, "David, I'm coming to your office. It's really urgent. I'm coming now." When he arrived he told David that his life was in danger. He said, "Look, we have three key witnesses and you're one of them. I don't know how to say this except to say we think that Dietrick is getting money from Vegas and that there are mob implications in this. There's been a politician killed in San Diego and we think it's all linked. We're giving you twenty-four-hour police protection."

David said no. When asked why, he explained, "Honestly I'd rather risk having bad guys follow me than to have police following me twenty-four hours a day. I'm not going to live like that. There's plenty of pressure as there is, and having to worry that someone is trying to kill me is just too much."

The other witnesses accepted the protection, and as it turned out there were no attempts to kill or injure the witnesses.

Before the grand jury made its decision, David took a short vacation trip to Hawaii to visit a friend. "When my friend picked me up at the airport, he said, 'David, today is the day. Aren't you nervous?' But I wasn't. There was nothing I could do. I felt I'd done what was right and I'd find out the verdict, and that would be that."

The verdict: Ralph Dietrick was indicted on fifty-eight counts of bribery and extortion. He was sentenced to two twenty-year terms and never returned to Orange County.

David became something of a hero in the community, but he insists that his greatest pleasure was in realizing that his actions had not only changed the nature of the business but had also changed the relationships between the developers and the community, a situation from which everyone as well as the environment benefited.

LESSONS TO REMEMBER

- Don't believe you have to play the game the way it has always been played, particularly if it's unfair.
- Challenge authority when it's wrong.
- Work with others for solutions that benefit everyone.
- Have the courage to condemn corruption for what it is.

FIRE SOMEONE YOU REALLY LIKE OR DO HER WORK YOURSELF?

*The only thing worse than a bad hire is bad
management of a bad hire.*

IF YOU'VE BEEN in management for any length of time, you've probably made a bad hire. You hired someone who impressed you in the interview or someone with whom you just seemed to have the right chemistry. In that situation, you probably didn't engage in the due diligence required to make a good hire: You didn't check references fully, you didn't scrutinize the work record, you didn't ask enough questions or the right questions. And why? Because you had a good impression, you liked the person, and you always trust your gut.

It's not a bad thing to use your intuition in evaluating potential employees, and perhaps most of the time things work out just fine. But if they don't, what then?

Well, it can go several ways. You know you should fire the person, but rather than face the pain of doing that, you try to adjust the job to fit his or her skills and talents. Of course, that leaves undone other job functions that someone else will have to do. And that someone else will probably resent it.

Or you transfer him or her to another job, if available. With luck, you'll find another manager who will take on your problem so you won't have to solve it.

Or you begin to do most of the work yourself in the hope that this employee you like so much will learn, respond, and start performing. These are common responses by managers to the hiring mistakes they've made. Sometimes these moves work, but most of the time they only make the situation worse. You end up frustrated, the employee feels frustrated and unappreciated, other employees become resentful, and the entire working environment begins to deteriorate.

Why? Because in your zeal to "save" this bad hire, a zeal you probably have justified by defining it as "doing the right thing" for this one person, you have done the wrong thing by your other employees, yourself, and your workplace.

This is the situation Bobbi Schlesinger found herself in as a relatively new manager several years ago. She had made a bad hire and then, she says, "It became more than a bad hire; it became bad management of a bad hire."

Bobbi heads a public relations agency in the New York City area, but at the time she was not the top person. Her job responsibilities were expanding rapidly, however, and she felt she needed another employee to take on some of the agency's work.

Anne (not her real name), one of the prospective employees she interviewed, was a very upbeat, impressive young woman, healthy and athletic looking, and enthusiastic. She was a writer but had not done public relations work. Bobbi was impressed enough with the conversation, however, that she felt the young woman could learn quickly, so she gave Anne the job.

Anne seemed to engage her responsibilities at the beginning, but to Bobbi's surprise and disappointment, her work never progressed and, in fact, it soon became mediocre.

"What it boiled down to," says Bobbi, "is that Anne simply was not interested in the work we do. She did not care about the subjects we cover and was not motivated to write about them."

Bobbi's response was fairly typical of many new managers. "I liked her a lot, so I thought it was my fault," she says. "I thought I just hadn't motivated her enough to get enthusiastic. In our work, we need to be able to write and speak enthusiastically. In fact, we need to be so enthusiastic about our subject that it becomes infectious and other people just get it.

"But Anne didn't get it, and it became clear that she didn't really want to get it."

So it was time for an appraisal and perhaps a probationary period. It was time to be clear about the consequences of not doing the job. But Bobbi rationalized that perhaps she could help by taking on some of the work herself, by demonstrating how it was to be done, by relieving Anne's load until she had a little more time and experience in the job. Bobbi also sometimes told herself that it was easier and more efficient just to do the job instead of taking time to push her employee to perform. Thus, rather than having her own workload relieved by hiring a person to help, Bobbi increased her load.

At about this time, a good friend showed her an article that made a big impact. "It explained how managers often take on their employees' burdens in the name of helping them, then the managers come to the end of the week and find that all the monkeys are on their back, the employees are off having a nice weekend, and I the manager never got to my own to-do list."

That same friend also made this observation—a good lesson for any manager: "The only thing worse than someone who quits and leaves is someone who quits and stays."

Bobbi doesn't remember the tipping point exactly, but she remembers coming to the realization that Anne was making her life much harder, and the situation was imposing on other employees as well. She realized also that, in her natural inclination to be supportive and compassionate toward the one person, she was not supporting the other people.

"It wasn't working, she wasn't helping me, and I knew I had to end it. But at the time I hadn't hired many people, and I'd never fired anyone. And here I was, about to fire someone I'd really come to like a great deal as a person. I thought about what to say and even rehearsed it a bit. Finally I got the courage to call her into the office, then I started by apologizing all over the place."

Apologizing? Bobbi explains that she still feels that in firing someone she should make it clear that somehow at least part of this is her fault.

"Then I said something like, 'Anne, I think we both know that this is not working. I don't think you're happy. I know I'm not happy with how it's going and I really don't think you're happy in this job.' At which point she agreed she was not happy.

"I think that by the time she came into the office, she understood that she was going to leave. There was no shock, no confrontation. In fact, we talked about how close we felt personally, and that only made me feel worse."

Whether it represents good management or not, Bobbi and Anne, in Bobbi's words, "wound up sitting on the floor crying, sharing a box of Kleenex, and saying things like, 'Oh God, this is horrible because we really like each other so much.'"

Clearly, Bobbi didn't know much at that point about firing people, and her lack of experience plus her affection for Anne made this episode not only very difficult but emotionally wrenching. Yet it also taught her some lasting lessons.

"I told Anne that she was in the wrong place and doing the wrong thing. I was very clear about that. I also told her that I felt she had some wonderful strengths, but that they just weren't right for this job. Then I talked about what she should be doing.

"And now when I have to fire people for inability to perform the job, I still use exactly that same conversation. But it has never gotten easier; it's always a difficult balancing act between concern for the individual and concern for our group. It probably won't get any easier either; that's why I'm now more careful about hiring."

LESSONS TO REMEMBER

- Understand that the best way to avoid firing someone is to be careful and thorough in the hiring process.
- Help your employees solve their problems, but don't solve their problems for them.
- Be sure you use all the good tools at your disposal, such as performance standards and appraisal procedures, in order to achieve complete clarity about job function and performance.
- Be aware of how one person's poor performance affects other employees' attitudes and causes morale problems.

THREE

SAY NO TO YOUR BIGGEST CUSTOMER OR GIVE UP ON FAIRNESS?

There's a moment of truth in every start-up business,
and it's always about money versus values.

ANYONE WHO HAS ever run a customer-sensitive business knows that customers come in four basic flavors: (1) reasonable, straightforward, and fair; (2) somewhat unpredictable and occasionally troublesome; and (3) often difficult and demanding. Then, of course, there's number 4: the bullies.

Doug Greene has faced several bully customers in his thirty years in business. "Difficult and demanding customers are never easy," he says, "but the first time I had to face a bully my whole business was at stake." Doug is now a prosperous entrepreneur, former CEO of New Hope Communications, which he founded and, a few years ago, sold. He served a term on the board of the acquiring company, plus he has businesses in this country and in Russia.

But Doug's story began in the garage of his home. He and his wife started a trade magazine called *Natural Foods Merchandiser* to serve the natural products industry. They risked everything to do it. "We offered our home up for the bank loan to print the first issue, and our ability to survive was limited at best. Every penny mattered. We had a tiny staff of part-timers, a couple of full-timers, plus my wife and I were working seventy hours a week with no money to pay ourselves a cent."

It was into this setting that Doug's biggest customer, the bully, let it be known that he was upset and that he wanted to talk immediately. "And he wanted to talk to me, the 'top dog.' I could feel the knot in my stomach tighten. This guy was always complaining about something and I wondered what it could be this time. To lose this customer would put me in a big trouble zone."

So Doug centered himself and made the call. He knew there was a big problem when the customer's assistant said, "Oh, I know he wants to talk with you immediately; let me get him out of his meeting."

Bob (not his real name) got right to the point: "Doug, I'm not happy with the story your people wrote in *Natural Foods Merchandiser*. You began the story by featuring one of our competitors, one that quite frankly doesn't advertise nearly as much as we do with you. Our company is much bigger and better, and you should have featured us. You are helping the competition and hurting us."

Balancing the coverage of an industry is one of the enduring challenges of magazines of all sizes. If one company is given more coverage than another, especially if the featured company is the biggest advertiser, there is the appearance of collusion and the magazine loses credibility with its readers. If that happens, the magazine is doomed. Unfortunately, there are magazine editors and publishers who are willing to sacrifice the reader connection and to risk their magazine's inevitable demise for short-term advertising revenues.

The temptation is always great to make the revenue statement look good now and worry about the long-term fallout later. This is true for CEOs as well as for profit center managers at all levels in a company. Doug, who had been a successful advertising salesman for another company, had vowed never to do this. "Our reasons for starting this company," he says, "were filled with good old-fashioned idealism. We wanted to help the nation's food supply get better, and we wanted to be able to have the same integrity in our business dealings that we wanted from the food supply."

He tried to explain this to the customer, but the bully wasn't buying it. "Doug, I want to know what you're going to do about it. We are ready to cancel all of our advertising immediately, and I doubt we will pay you for anything we owe you until we talk with our attorney about the damages you've done to us."

It is very unlikely that, in the media world, an advertiser will bring a lawsuit claiming damages because a magazine featured a competitor in an editorial article, particularly if the complaining company was not even mentioned in the article, much less compared unfavorably to the company that was featured. In this case, there was no issue of libel. The advertiser was just angry because his competitor got some coverage.

Doug knew he was on safe legal grounds, but he was aware that lawsuits often have nothing to do with legal grounds and more to do with pushing and shoving to a conclusion. Doug also knew he could not afford a lawsuit, but he felt all he could do was hold firm.

"I was dealing with an important industry player," he says, "a guy who was used to getting what he wanted because other magazines had already given in to his bullying. Also, I knew that by the time he got to me, he had verbally abused and threatened a couple of our employees."

Doug decided to make another try at reason and explanation. He began, "Bob, I understand that you're upset and you're right in noting that the article you mentioned is an important article, but our writer was more focused on what's happening rather than on who is advertising. That's what gives us credibility with our readers and your customers . . ."

The bully did not let him finish. "Doug," he shouted into the phone, "I don't give a damn about your so-called credibility. I want to hear about how you're going to make it up to me if you want to do business with us. I want a major story on our company. You owe us. And I don't want to see a competitor mentioned ahead of us again."

Clearly, Doug thought, this guy is very used to getting his way. "I could just see the ads canceling and hear him slandering us to his industry friends as 'not professional,' and so on."

Listening patiently, Doug glanced around the crowded room above his garage where the staff was, as usual, working beyond what anyone had the right to expect. They were doing it because they believed in the mission and they believed in Doug. To give in to the bully customer might help the finances, but it would be breaking faith with his people and with his own vision of a company that gives all its customers special treatment and never plays one over the others.

At that moment Doug became calm. "I realized then that we had to draw the line and let fairness and kindness be our guide even at the risk to our financial well-being. I knew that I was going to have to go directly against what Bob was trying to get me to do, but that if I said it with any of the same anger and force that he'd used on me, my delivery would detract from my message."

Doug took a deep breath and began: "Bob, you are an important person in our industry and your company is a proven leader. We very much like having a relationship with you and your business is important to us.

"We're trying our best to bring much-needed good information to our industry. I admit that sometimes we do it better than other times, but we have a high sense of purpose and passion here, and one of our core values is how we like to be fair to everyone, big and small.

"We do not do feature stories on supplier companies because our focus is more on the retail side of the business, and we find the readers don't want company profiles, they want fresh information on what is happening and why. Our readers are your customers, so I hope you feel our work is good enough to earn part of your advertising budget."

Doug was feeling good about the speech, but it was as if Bob had been holding his breath until he could speak. His hostility almost crackled through the phone as he shouted, "Don't give me all this bullshit about relationships. I want a feature story to make up for what you did to me, and I want it now. Cancel all our advertising immediately. When you see what you can do for us, then we'll consider where we are with you, but don't expect any payments. You owe us!"

Doug had heard from other publishers about these kinds of run-ins in the industry, and he'd come to realize that wheeling and dealing, along with threatening, had been a common industry practice. It certainly would have been easy for Doug to say yes, get off the phone, and do an article. But there would then have been no end to the unreasonable demands of those who wanted to create the media policies for wherever they advertised.

So Doug tried again: "Bob, we really want to do business with you, you're an important company . . ."

Click. The phone went dead. When Doug replaced the receiver, he became aware that everyone in his office was tuned into the drama going on around this advertiser. There had been flare-ups before, but nothing like this.

Doug faced an almost classic decision between what was in his short-term interest versus what would be best in the long term. It is difficult to imagine anyone in a leadership position for very long who has not been faced with some version of this age-old conflict. In Doug's case, his very business depended on his decision. We can almost hear what must have gone through his head as a possible justification: *I have to do this or I could lose the whole business. Yes, the guy is a jerk and treated my staff poorly, but if he stiffs me, they may all be out of a job and what good is that?*

"We had said nothing bad about his company," Doug explains. "We only mentioned a very small competitor in a normal story. It was a case of finding ourselves in the crosshairs of a control freak. Our standing up to him had lit his fuse, and I couldn't imagine what the blowup would be."

Then there came the practical decision about the advertising. "We were one day away from sending the current issue to the printer and we had Bob's full-page ad in the issue. Did we run it or not? We were close to break-even on this issue, and the loss of this one ad would put us in the red."

The next morning Doug realized he had no choice but to try to reason with Bob one more time. "I reminded myself that we could do a few extra things for him, make a few promises privately, and things would be back on track until his next hunger attack. But it would not be fair, and how would I ever be able to look key industry members in the eye knowing that I had sold out my fairness standard and let all of this integrity business we were pushing be compromised by a large pushy customer?"

Doug made the call, and when Bob answered with, "Good morning, Doug, I hope you've come to your senses," Doug knew he was still in trouble. Nonetheless he made his speech, explaining that "what I can do for you, Bob, is promise that I will always be fair to you and that you can expect that we are not playing favorites anywhere. Your company will always have access to everything that anyone gets."

It was a good, high-minded beginning but was quickly interrupted. "Doug, you must not have heard me yesterday. We want an article. In fact, I've already told my people to expect it or to drop you completely."

Doug, the good salesman he'd been trained to be, decided to finish his speech anyway. "Bob, your company is very important, and we also hope to become an important company, and I can promise you that we will strive in every way we can to help you, but I cannot back off our fairness rule. I hope you'll reconsider and I think you'll find we're by far the best value for your advertising budget. We dearly want to have a good long-term relationship with you."

"Doug, I think I've heard enough."

Click.

At this point, almost anyone's inclination would be to think something like, "I don't need this, I don't have time for this, let me choose to just get this conflict behind me."

A compelling thought, indeed, but choosing this path can become a very slippery slope that has all kinds of unintended consequences. There was likely another voice inside Doug, asking these tough questions: *"What about the integrity and values that I want to build this business on? What will caving in to this guy say to my staff? And if I give in to him this time, what will he demand of me next time?"*

This conflict with an important customer and industry player was, for Doug and his infant company, a critical "tipping point" experience that would determine the very future of the organization.

Doug's sinking feeling of the previous day returned as he tried to decide whether to run the ad in the current issue now going to the printer or to pull it. He decided to leave the ad in the magazine, concluding that "even if Bob's company pulled out, they could at least see that even in a fight we were trying to make peace and get our relationship back on track."

In the midst of Doug's worries came an immediate and unexpected response from his team, who'd been watching the situation through days of hard work bordering on burnout. Suddenly they rallied with a newfound deeper spirit. They realized, as Doug put it, "that this integrity talk was real and they'd found a place to work they could be proud of." Doug decided then and there that compassion, professionalism, and integrity would always be celebrated in his company.

Then the big surprise. The next morning, someone from Bob's office called and said they wanted to continue their advertising.

"We were shocked," Doug says. "Bob did not call back himself, and it was several months before I ran into him at an industry gathering. I was amazed at how nice he was, treating me now as a peer rather than just a media vendor. He said he hoped we could figure out more ways to work together."

Doug points out that Bob's company ended up being one of his top ten clients and "one we greatly enjoyed working with." Doug can't explain the turnaround exactly, but he knows it had something to do with sticking to his policy of integrity, patience, fairness, and compassion.

Doug's publication went on to become, far and away, the largest and most respected publication in the business.

Doug's story had a happy ending, but it could have gone the other way. It is critical that leaders understand the long-term and short-term implications of their possible choices, and to understand that the implications are not just about money but also about vision and values. If there is a choice to be made that is good both in the short term and long term, then it is obviously the right choice. More often than not, it's not that easy or obvious.

No amount of financial analysis could have made the "right choice" obvious for Doug. He was running the great risk that his fledgling magazine could lose the advertising support of one the industry's biggest players. On the other hand, for years he had heard complaints about industry publications that were so compliant to the demands of their big advertisers that the publications became little more than promotional brochures. He was determined to create a magazine to serve the entire industry, which he knew would also serve his advertisers.

His gut told him that even if the bully canceled his advertising, other advertisers would admire the magazine's demonstrated independence and would support him. Whether or not he could achieve a comfortable level of profitability without this one dominant advertiser was the unanswerable question. But he was sure of one thing: If he gave in, then his magazine would become an also-ran, just another sellout publication in the world of sellout publications. He could avoid the present crisis, save his business and his staff's jobs, but he would never be able to create a dominant position and he'd probably find himself struggling to stay in business with a magazine he wasn't proud of.

Understand that Doug's dilemma was not just about money and the business. It was about his own vision and about his sense of integrity. His struggle was like so many in organizational life. It was internal, and while he could get advice from others and while he could think through the possible scenarios and consequences, his choice was about the kind of person in business he wanted to be, not the amount of business he wanted to do; it was about creating a unique medium, not about caretaking just another trade journal; and, finally, it was about human values, not dollar values.

It requires courage to choose your vision with confidence that it is best in the long term; you have to overcome fear about the short-term sacrifices you may incur, but courage is a trait of effective leaders. Especially in times of conflict, the leader must keep the vision of the business and the core values in mind.

With hindsight, it's easy for anyone to see that Doug made the right choice. At the time, however, he had to summon the courage to act in concert with his values and to recognize that this is always in the long-term interest, regardless of possible short-term consequences. However, he also enjoyed some immediate benefits. His actions said to his staff, "I walk my talk. I will be consistent and true to my values even under pressure." It is so empowering and inspiring to employees when they see their leaders acting from a place of integrity.

There were other immediate benefits as well. Doug did get paid, did not lose an important customer as he feared, and also gained the respect of one of his key customers. Most important, he was at peace. He made the tough choice, but he did what he knew in his heart was right.

LESSONS TO REMEMBER

- Appreciate the long-term effect of doing what you say you're going to do.
- Remain calm and courteous even in the face of anger and verbal abuse.
- Never let yourself be driven by the fear of failure.
- Don't sacrifice your peace of mind for a short-term solution.

FOUR

DO THE RIGHT THING IMMEDIATELY OR POSTPONE IT FOR THE GREATER GOOD?

*Sometimes there is just no "right" choice and you are
required to deal with what's most right or what's most
wrong.*

THERE IS A monument at the U.S. Military Academy at West
Point called the "honor code monument." George Pierson
(not his real name), a graduate and veteran of Desert Storm,
now CEO of Wild Spring Organics (a fictitious company
name), a natural personal care products company, still visits
that special spot on the West Point campus whenever he's in
the area. He sits quietly and reflects on how the code now ap-
plies to his life in business.

"I go there to recharge my integrity batteries," he says.
"The code says that a cadet will not lie, cheat, or steal, or tolerate those who do, and what I've faced in business these
past couple of years has put me to the test particularly when
it comes to the part about tolerating those who do."

While George felt that in his army service compromising
his integrity was never an option, his business experiences
have made him realize that there are differences between ac-

curacy and truth, that long-term ethical concerns can at times trump short-term accuracy, that compassion and fair dealing can outweigh rigid definitions of integrity. The circumstances are rarely as black-and-white as the ones he faced on combat patrol.

George's story begins when he joined the board of Wild Spring Organics. The company had been purchased by a private equity group that prided itself on integrity and honest operating principles. After the purchase, it started to become apparent to the new owners and members of the board, including George, that things were not always as they had been characterized by the original owners.

"Some of the words and pictures just didn't match," George says, "but it wasn't obvious at first to me and other board members what the issues were or the depth of the problems we were soon to face."

Six months later, George was recruited to take the CEO position and joined the company full-time. "I suspected there were problems I would have to address, but if I had known the extent of the issues and what I was getting into," George says, "I might have just walked away from the opportunity. But I knew and trusted people on the board, and believed in the opportunity with the company. I was confident the board would support whatever we needed to do to fix any problems."

The problem George first discovered was evidence of financial manipulation. "Inaccuracy and inconsistency were rampant within the company, and this lead to perceived lack of integrity—perceived, that is, by the employees. And for good reason.

"For instance, someone might make the decision to input

the cost of goods on an item at $1.95, then when the profit-and-loss statement was run it was discovered that there was no profit on that item. Rather than honestly address the problem, whether it was pricing, cost of production, or sales, the prior owners would instruct their staff to just change the cost of goods to $1.75, to show a profit of $0.20. Quite simply, they were cooking the books.

"And that wasn't all. There were issues of unpaid taxes and accounting irregularities, loans off the books to family members, all kinds of potentially embarrassing, damaging, and in some cases illegal activities."

One of George's first actions was to write the following letter to all of the company's employees. He knew he needed to radically change the culture in the company and establish an imperative of trust, honesty, and integrity in how they conducted business. This is how he started that process.

To all employees:

I have developed my leadership philosophy over the years to guide my actions. I strive to live and work according to these principles. I share them with you, my co-workers, so you'll know the basis for my actions and so that you can let me know when I'm falling short of these goals.

My job is to ensure that we accomplish our company's goals, improving the organization, and supporting our team as they try to realize their full potential. In influencing those results, it is imperative that I provide the team with purpose, direction, and motivation.

My goal is to have happy customers and happy employees. Customers are happy when they get good products and services for a fair price. Employees are happy when they have some control over their work and their careers, when they are engaged in meaningful work and are treated with respect. I will be concerned with both people and results.

I believe that people want to succeed; my job is to create an environment where that can happen.

I will tell the truth, and I expect others to tell the truth. This includes bringing me the bad news, when it is fresh, when we can still act on it. Bad news can still be good data.

I will have the moral courage to make the tough calls. If I can't figure out what the right thing is on my own, I will ask for help. When I do make a decision on a sensitive matter, I'll be willing to explain myself.

I will keep in mind that you have interests and obligations outside of work. To the extent that I can make these aspects of your life fit together well, I will. In return, I expect you to work hard and smart.

I will actively seek input and advice. Give me your honest counsel. If I don't think to ask, give it to me anyway.

If I see you do something or hear of a decision you make that is ethically questionable, I will ask you about it. Don't be offended. When you see me do something that you are unsure of, ask me and I'll explain myself. I won't be offended. We will make ethical decisions if we are willing to shine light into those dark corners, if we are willing to challenge ourselves and each other.

I will keep my sense of humor, and so should you. I will keep a cheerful outlook, especially in tough times. I will be energetic.

I will take responsibility for my actions, and so should you. We all make mistakes. We will all try to learn from our mistakes.

When assigning projects, I will try to balance your need to try new things and learn new skills with the customers' needs for the best products and services that we can deliver.

Finish your projects on time. If you can't, let someone know as soon as you figure that out.

Communication is the key to smooth operations and to building trust. We must make our concerns known and share feedback throughout the organization. We will be honest, and we will not indulge in personal attacks.

My hot buttons:

If you lie to me or steal from the company or a customer, I will fire you.

Be on time and prepared for meetings.

Don't gossip.

Don't whine.

Don't just point out problems; propose solutions.

Do the right thing. Develop your action plan before you get into a crisis.

Guard your integrity like it is your most precious possession.

Live in the Learning Zone. Get out of the Comfort Zone.

Read ten minutes a day.

Listen to people.

Give back.

Set goals (and hold yourself accountable).

Stay positive.

Several key employees responded very positively to the letter. They felt safe enough to go to him and expose a new problem that was to become the greatest challenge George had faced in his career, not only to his management skills, but to his integrity as well. That's when he learned about the labeling problem.

"The financial stuff going on in the company was fairly easily fixable," George says, "but when I learned of our labeling problem, I was faced with the harshest reality I could imagine. The problem can be stated very simply: The company was mislabeling its products. Put another way, the company was lying about the ingredients and formulations listed on its labels.

"For instance," George explains, "we were distributing an organic rosemary soap with no organic rosemary in the product, only an artificial rosemary fragrance. Unfortunately, I discovered that we had several hundred items in the market and several hundred incorrect labels. What was on the label was not in the product, and we had ingredients in the product that were not on the label." These mislabeled products were on the shelves of natural foods stores throughout the country.

So George faced two hard choices: what to do in order to fix the products and also what action to take against the prior owners, who had created this mess and still were 20 percent owners of the company. George immediately notified the board of the issues. He knew that fixing the labeling issue was an urgent and important operational issue, but one management was responsible for fixing. However, the decision whether or not to pursue legal recourse against the prior owners was a board decision and not his alone. George posed this question to the board: "What should be done about the people who left us with this mess? Shouldn't we sue them, shouldn't we seek some recompense for their patently unethical activities, for their misrepresentations to us when we bought the company, and for what we're having to go through to fix it?"

These were reasonable questions by any measurement. Any board or management group would be tempted to seek a legal remedy, and it was clear that the facts in this case supported the chances of prevailing in court. So why not sue?

The answer was as simple as it was dramatic. Were legal action pursued, then the labeling and product integrity issue would become public knowledge. Surely, this would have been reported in the trade press and once the natural foods stores throughout the country learned of the labeling problem, the products would be pulled off the shelves immediately and immeasurable damage done to the credibility of the brand. "Pursuing a lawsuit would have taken years and ultimately, I have no doubt, we would have prevailed, but in the process I don't think the company would have survived. As much as we wanted justice, the costs of achieving it were simply too high."

Choking back a lot of anger, George and the board decided to forgo whatever recompense might be realized in a lawsuit but were committed to getting the prior owners completely out of the business. They still owned 20 percent of the company, and it was a completely untenable situation to still have them around. Furthermore, having them participate in the future success of the company was simply unfathomable. So what did George and the board decide to do?

"We had to negotiate to buy out their remaining interest in

the business. We ended up having to write a check for a few million dollars to the people who had, in effect, defrauded us, and it really stuck in my craw," says George. "But as difficult as it was, I realized it would have cost much more had we made the company successful then bought them out later. We had to end their involvement, and this was the only way to accomplish that without involving the courts."

George's next hard choice was operational. Now he and his people took on the daunting task of fixing the labeling problems. Many of the products were mislabeled and in some cases ineffective. This needed to be rectified, but how could they do so without completely destroying the company's image and brand in the process? They considered recalling all the products, but as one board member put it, "the cure would be worse than the disease," because while it would correct the situation, it could quite possibly take the company under and in the process put a lot of people out of work. It would hurt people who had put their lives into trying to make the company good, and it would hurt investors and vendors.

"That would have been an action of one hundred percent integrity," George says, "but we'd have no business left when we were done." And George and the board felt strongly that the company had a very bright future once this problem was resolved. If the product line could be cleaned up and positioned properly, Wild Spring Organics would be a great company.

Since a total recall was not a viable solution, what was next? George recalls: "The first thing we asked ourselves was if there were any safety issues with any of these mislabeled products." We were looking for a reasonable rationale to apply to the situation, and consumer safety was it. There might not have been any organic rosemary in the shampoo, but no one was going to be harmed by using our product. It was a safe product; it just wasn't what our consumers thought it was. Would I call what we decided to do one hundred percent honest? Probably not, but that is what made the situation such a hard choice. I had to balance these questions with my fiduciary responsibilities. This was a very complex problem with no easy answers. The fact is that there were no safety issues involved, so we decided a total recall wasn't necessary. But we also felt we had to correct the situation as soon as was humanly possible."

The next step was to assess the financial impact of relabeling the product and establish as tight a timetable as possible for fixing the problem. "We quantified what we were going to write off. We determined which products could be fixed and discontinued those that we could not. In some cases it was as simple as just putting what was on the label in the product. We attacked the most serious issues first, and vowed that we were going to have a completely clean product line, everything correct—labels, ingredients, everything—in six months."

This was an incredibly short deadline. George took this plan to the employees. "I feared losing credibility with the employees because we were leaving some mislabeled products in the marketplace during the transition, but I knew they also realized that a recall could cost them their jobs. What they really needed was a mile marker, a timetable for success.

"We also laid out the entire plan for them, complete transparency. Every single employee knew what we were doing and what it was going to cost to do it.

"Everyone knew their role, from the guy picking the orders or receiving the materials into the warehouse to the person who was changing the labels to the accountants who were doing the bookkeeping. We not only had to fix the labels, we had to get the financial statements accurate."

And how did the employees respond?

"We got it all done in six months, which was a lot of sleepless nights for a lot of people. But they did it willingly because they knew it was the right thing to do and they understood what the stakes were.

"And in the process we took a big hit to earnings, but we saved the company and the brand."

The results of all of this have been very good. Even with far fewer products in the marketplace, sales were up 20 percent in the last year. Reflecting on the situation a year later, George commented: "As difficult as the whole situation was, I have no doubt we are a stronger company today because of what we went through as a team. Our product line today is now the standard of the industry."

There is always more work to do, of course, and George still has one big personal issue to overcome. "I'm still pissed at the original owners who did all this," he says, "but I try to remember that they did some good things as well. And I am so grateful to the employees who worked so hard to help make the company into what we want it to be."

Still, for George, it all goes back to that monument at West Point, and he has found it particularly difficult to "tolerate those" who violate the code. "The true definition of integrity," he says, "is that you will do what you say you're going to do," then he pauses and adds, "and you'll still do it when no one is looking."

LESSONS TO REMEMBER

- Think long-term. Sometimes doing the perfectly right thing now will be the wrong thing later.
- Let your people know your philosophy and values right up front.
- Don't keep crises to yourself. Share the problem, ask your people for help, and they can work a miracle.
- Understand that seeking retribution, while personally satisfying, may only make the problems worse.

GO FOR THE QUICK FIX OR
TEACH VALUES FIRST?

Turnaround artists are supposed to cut, slash, and
burn. Right?

YOU COULD CALL Tim Tuff a turnaround artist* but he
doesn't fit the mold of all those other CEOs we've read about,
the ones who ride in with their saddlebags full of tricks and
their eyes focused on a short-term solution.

Not that Tim criticizes those CEOs. "I'm sure there are people better than I am in those gut-wrenching turnaround situations," he says, "and I'm sure there are people better than I
am in growth situations. I tend to navigate that bend in the
river. Yes, I've spent most of my life, actually, in turnaround
situations, with companies that have lost their way. I try to do
the turnaround, then take them on into growth situations. A
little of both."

Tim is suspicious of anyone who walks in with a tool kit, a
ready-made solution for any situation. "My experience is that

---

*A top manager, usually a CEO, who specializes in taking over companies
that are unprofitable and returning them to profitability.

every situation is different. I don't have a set plan or a tool kit, and I don't walk in with my team of the same people for every company. I've found good people everywhere, but they just haven't been given the right direction."

Tim describes his approach as something like "creating a revolution" in that he believes the first step is winning the hearts and minds of the people in the company.

"When I move into a turnaround situation, it's like moving into a raging fire, and everyone feels pressured to do things expediently; I normally blow the whistle and say, 'Hang on. Let's establish some ground rules. I know we have dissatisfied customers. We've got highly dissatisfied shareholders. And everybody's totally overworked. But let's first sort out how we're going to go about business.' Normally in these situations, the seas are very choppy and it's very difficult for people to see what is acceptable and what is not."

At this point, Tim lays out the values and tries to get a clear understanding of those values. "It's one thing to say 'integrity,' but you need to lay out the ground rules and then be very consistent."

While the words he uses may be different in different organizations, his essential values remain the same.

"It always starts with respect, and that means respect even under pressure," he says. "You have to respect everyone you deal with: employees, customers, vendors, the community, everyone. It takes more time to treat people with respect, and when you are under pressure, it seems counterintuitive to insist on something that takes more time. But without the value of respect, nothing else works.

"Of course you can always try the quick fix, but most of these companies didn't get into a mess overnight. You can apply the Band-Aid if you're just planning to flip the business, but I'm not looking to do that. I'm looking to provide a foundation for growth. So if you're planning to really turn the business around you've got to start with the basics. No turnaround will be lasting unless you start with the basics. And I think there has got to be leadership by example."

In Tim's hierarchy of values, respect leads to the next essential aspect of integrity, trust. "I think when you're moving into a mess, you have to establish trust very fast. Don't get hung up on strategy. In a turnaround, people are often running around bumping into each other, and what you need to do is tell them which corner of the room they're heading for. You really don't need to be more precise than that. You need to give people a framework for decision-making because normally I find that people are afraid of making decisions. You've got to get decision-making as close to the customer as possible. That requires trust.

"And you can't establish trust without also committing to being open and honest. I mean brutally open and honest. Admit if you make a mistake. I say, when in doubt, tell the truth always. And don't just tell what is factually correct; there's often a difference between accuracy and truth. Tell me the way it really is."

But don't people fear that the messenger of bad news may be shot? How does Tim avoid that?

"By the consistency of my actions. I think part of it is putting people at ease and also never betraying a confidence. And always reinforce recognition of people who behave according to the values."

What about those who don't behave according to the values? Tim feels that management actions often have both a pragmatic and a symbolic aspect, and that the company's values can be communicated most effectively by demonstrating the consequences of violating those values.

"I remember one situation, again this was a turnaround. I had one plant that was operating really well with a very bright, competent young manager. He was clearly an outstanding performer. But one of the employees said he had made a racially biased comment. I said, 'We'll investigate it.' One of my managers asked me, 'Why on earth with all the whole suite of problems you have on your desk, would you ask someone to spend any time investigating something like that of the one manager who knows what the hell he's doing?'

"And I said, 'Because it is fundamentally contrary to respect and we will not tolerate it irrespective of who or how good the person is.' "

The inspector made his report: Yes, the manager had made the comment. Tim's response: "Fire him. I've explained the values to him, so it's not as if he didn't know."

On the surface, this may seem overly harsh. Couldn't the man have been reprimanded, then given some sensitivity training and another chance? And, as one of Tim's managers asked, why would Tim focus on this incident with everything else there was to do? Yes, it would certainly have been an option to give the man some training and then give him another chance, and yes, Tim had more than enough to focus on. But the answer to both those questions lies in Tim's belief that getting the values right and achieving an understanding of the ground rules are vital first steps to success. To make a rule stick, to demonstrate the commitment to a value—in this case, the value of respect—sometimes requires a zero-tolerance approach. To let the manager get by with even one disrespectful act or comment would have sent the message that there really is "wiggle room" when it comes to the values.

So they fired the manager with the best record in the company. The word spread through the company quickly and, according to Tim, the employees said, "My God, if he fires him, I better take this seriously."

Tim credits the symbolism of this action with helping move the company forward. "If you were looking for short-term expedience, you would never have done that," he says, "but let me tell you, if you are serious about getting the ship righted, then really moving forward, this is definitely the way to do it."

Tim is just as adamant about the core value of safety. "Safety trumps everything else in a plant," he says, then he tells the story of another turnaround situation involving an action that few managers would ever consider.

"Normally, I find that the people who have been the most abused and are having the toughest time are the people on the front line. We had a concrete tile business in Arizona, and we were getting enormous complaints from customers. So I visited some of the customers and listened to their concerns. The product was inconsistent; there was a lot of breakage; turnaround times were awful; and we were way behind on our deliveries.

"So next I visited the plant. It was horrendous for safety. The people in the plant were not properly equipped. There were forklifts being operated by people who had not been trained, and I witnessed a close call in which someone could have been killed or seriously injured.

"So I said to the plant manager, 'You know, safety is one of our values and if we can't operate a plant safely we shouldn't operate it.' He said, 'Look, I understand, but we haven't been inspected and we're way behind on deliveries. I just need to catch up; then I'll give the people the training.' "

At that point, Tim did something he doesn't usually do: He intervened directly in the management of the plant. He said to the manager, "You know what? You're not going to get caught up first. I don't often make these kinds of decisions, but what I've seen is unsafe, period. We've been very lucky so far. So stop the plant right now."

But didn't that mean losing orders, revenue, and probably customers? It did. But Tim told the manager that he should provide the training quickly, then he said, "Before you start out, I want you to actually invite OSHA [Occupational Hazards and Safety Administration inspectors] into the plant and get them to help you get this plant running safely."

The plant was shut down, the maintenance done on the equipment, the people trained, and the place cleaned up.

The impact? "First, we lost a big chunk of business, and at the time we were in great financial distress, but it sent a message all across the organization to all forty or so plants. And suddenly the first thing I'd hear about when I walked into a plant was the safety. I always said the most difficult thing to manage is safety, and if you've got a plant that's operating very safely, you'll find that everything else is being operated very well, too."

While safety in itself is a core value of Tim's, he also relates it back to the value of respect. "It comes out of respect for your colleagues. Would you ask your spouse or your brother to go to work in a plant where they might get injured? I don't think so. Why on earth then would you ask a fellow worker to do that?"

Another core value, and one that also often requires some hard choices, is diversity. Tim points out that he has run businesses in twenty different countries, and that he has always operated with a fundamental view that his workforce should be as representative as possible of the community and that the management should be as representative as possible of the workforce, insisting that employees should find people like themselves in management.

He recalls another turnaround situation, in which the management team recommended closing a clay tile plant that was suffering major losses. He told the team that he wanted to visit the plant.

"They said, 'Hang on, we just said we're recommending closing it.' And I said, 'Well, you can recommend closing it, but I still want to see it because I always learn something going around a plant.'

"So I went out to the plant on my own and you could see there was just incredible amounts of scrap being produced. And there was one person working really hard pulling all of these broken tiles off the belt and throwing them in the scrap pile. It was actually very hard work. He was Hispanic, so I spoke to him in Spanish.

"I said, 'I'm the new guy on the block. I see you producing all this scrap. Why are you just continuing to run the machine? Why not stop the machine because you're having to work really hard getting rid of fifty percent of this stuff?'

"The man told me it was because they won't pay for maintaining the dye. And I asked what was involved in that, and he showed me a very simple fix. I asked how much that would cost and he said, 'About fifty to one hundred bucks.' "

Tim then discovered that the worker had not been able to

suggest the change because he didn't speak English and the plant manager didn't speak Spanish. Not only that, no one on the plant management team spoke Spanish.

Tim went back to the manager and asked what would happen if we fixed the dye as the worker had suggested. The manager said he didn't think it would work. So Tim asked, "Would you do me a favor? Would you try it?" The plant manager said again that he didn't think it would work.

"So I took someone from another plant," Tim recalls, "and asked him to go supervise a trial. It worked."

What Tim faced was a dramatic example of how management's attention to the workers closest to the process would have prevented a major problem. But how could managers pay attention when they couldn't even communicate with the people most responsible for producing the product? So it was also an example of how a lack of appropriate diversity could have killed an entire operation.

Tim made a choice. "One month later, I went back to the plant and actually fired the whole management crew. I brought in someone who, though he had never been in that business before, was bilingual and told him to go at it. He got that business turned around and today it's the largest clay tile producer in the United States." This sent yet another strong signal to the rest of Tim's company.

The lesson is that the people closest to the product and the process are most likely to know how things work and what to do. But most executives are reluctant to make choices that support the people on the line. It's always easier to make rules, to look over people's shoulders, to turn the management team into a group of enforcers rather than enablers.

"I mean, again, people are not stupid and they should not be treated that way," says Tim. "Look, it takes time to build trust, to operate by these values. It takes longer in terms of demonstrating results, and of course there is enormous pressure in a turnaround to get the cash flowing. But you just have to take risks on behalf of the workforce. You can have thousands of people working for you, and if they realize that your values are aligned with theirs, they will work their asses off to help you."

LESSONS TO REMEMBER

- Understand the importance of making your values known as soon as you can.
- Ensure that your employees can be heard and understood, regardless of language barriers.
- Lead by example.
- Don't try quick fixes for problems that took a long time to develop.
- Don't underestimate the value of talking to the people on the front lines.

DO WHAT EVERYBODY'S DOING OR
DO WHAT YOU KNOW IS RIGHT?

When the boss insists that you cheat, what then?

ERIC PETERSEN (not his real name) felt he had been given the chance of a lifetime when he was hired onto the staff of a national magazine. He'd been out of college less than three years and had worked first as a freelance writer and then as a staff member of a small regional publication that he quickly discovered was a hand-to-mouth operation, barely surviving from one issue to the next.

He knew he was fortunate to be given a chance in what he thought of as the "big-time publishing business," even though he was starting in a job he could only describe to his friends as "low man on the totem pole." Still, it was an opportunity to prove himself, and there would be no place to go but up.

The transition was a bit of a shock. He was warmly received, but the environment and working habits were so different from his admittedly limited experience in the other company that it felt almost extravagant to him. At the small publication, he had done whatever needed to be done—make coffee, run errands, sell office supplies in the front office, even change the paper towels in the restrooms—but in this new place each person seemed to have one thing, and only one thing, to do.

Whereas he had been accustomed to packing his own lunch and eating at his desk, everyone here went to a restaurant for lunch. After a couple of weeks, it became clear that people here did not pack their own lunches. Also, he began to feel he was missing a chance to socialize with the other staff members, so even though he knew that a restaurant lunch would be an expense he hadn't budgeted for, he decided to join the group. Then another shock: He discovered that the others charged the meals to their expense accounts. "We've been talking business," one of them explained, "so we consider this a staff conference. It's perfectly legal."

Eric was intensely aware that he was from a small town and younger than most of the others, but he did not consider himself an utterly naive, clueless hick; however, he was afraid that his new colleagues might think of him that way if he did not do as they did. So he accepted their word on the "staff conference" and didn't question it further. And they did talk business; of course they always seemed to talk nothing but business anyway, wherever they were.

"At the time I thought that maybe this is just the norm for a big magazine like this," Eric says now. "I just didn't have enough experience to be able to evaluate the huge culture change I was going through."

In the next several months Eric continued to go along with whatever the norm seemed to be, even though the expense-paid lunches struck him as excessive. "I was raised to be very prudent with money," he says, "and I was sometimes astonished by how much company money would be spent for personal lunches and drinks.

"But," he adds, smiling, "it was also a bit dazzling for this small-town kid. I remember thinking that this must be the way they do it in the big time. I certainly didn't complain."

One day the managing editor called Eric into the office and explained about a new series the magazine was going to do featuring regional travel tours in the United States.

"To begin, we're sending writers to four different regions," the managing editor said, "and because you came from the Midwest and wrote for a regional pub, I want you to take about ten days and bring back a couple of good stories on driving tours around the Midwest. Do one east of the Mississippi and one west of the Mississippi. And avoid the big cities. We want to get a real feel of the country."

What a terrific assignment. This is what every young staff writer dreams of doing, and Eric was effusive in thanking his boss. Eric would be going to his home territory and not only just writing about it but doing so in a way that would intrigue other people to follow his route.

Eric spent eleven days on the road and brought back not two but three good pieces. The managing editor was delighted.

Then came the chore every businessperson has to do from time to time: the expense report. Eric carefully assembled the receipts and turned in the report to his direct supervisor, a department head, who would then forward it to the managing editor and on to the accounting department.

The next day, the department head called Eric into his office.

"Eric," he said, "I need to talk to you about your expense report."

Eric was alarmed. He'd done it correctly, included receipts, and accounted for every expenditure. What could be wrong?

The department head motioned him around the desk so they could study the reports together. Eric was astonished to see big red circles around some of the meal expenses and a couple of the motel bills, and there was a big check mark where Eric had left a blank space.

"Let's start here," his boss said, pointing to the blank. "Why is there no expenditure here?" he asked.

"I spent that night in Mason City, Iowa," Eric said, "and my old college roommate lives there, so I stayed with him and his family. It didn't cost anything."

"Okay," said the department head, "but even these hotel bills look cheaper than they should."

Eric explained that he had stayed in small-town motels and, by city standards, they were very inexpensive.

His boss nodded and ran his finger down the expenses, stopping at the red circles he'd made around the meal expenses. Finally he said, "Eric, I appreciate that you want to save the company money by living as inexpensively as you can while traveling, but this is just unacceptable."

"Sir?" Eric replied. "I don't understand."

"It's simple. We expect our editors and writers to have a certain public image when they travel. When you stay in inexpensive motels, eat at fast-food places, and so on, you send the message that we—that the magazine—can't afford better. It's a bad image."

"It seemed a reasonable explanation," Eric recalls. "I could see that there might be a public image problem, but then he said something that made me wonder if this was company policy or just an editorial department practice."

The boss said, "Not only is there the image problem, but when you travel this cheaply, you make everyone else's expense reports look expensive. Next thing you know, the accounting people are wondering why we don't all travel this cheap. Then we'd have real problems."

"What kind of problems?" Eric asked.

"Morale problems, of course. These are creative people. They'd feel they were being squeezed by the bean counters in accounting, who are just jealous anyway of anyone who gets to travel on an expense account."

Eric did not know what to say, so he waited until the boss spoke again.

"So, Eric, take these reports back and jack up the expenses. You can't do that with the motel bills because there are receipts, but you don't need receipts for any meal up to twenty-five dollars, so just increase the cost of meals up to twenty-five dollars. Throw in some tips or laundry expenses, incidentals. Like that. You can probably add a few hundred dollars that way."

He handed the reports to Eric, who, as he recalls, just said "Okay" and left the office. He had gone along with the expense account lunches, but now he was being asked, or more accurately, ordered to falsify expense reports. And the order was characterized as if he would be doing something wrong not to comply.

Eric did not know whether what he was being told to do was illegal, but he knew it was wrong. On one hand, he could refuse, but that would mean confronting his boss or going over his head to the managing editor, who, for all Eric knew, would feel the same way about his expense reports. On the other hand, this was a big multimillion-dollar operation and what difference would a few hundred dollars make, particularly if making the changes would avoid a confrontation? They wouldn't even be noticed. And of course, Eric would be reimbursed for the expenses that he didn't incur, so he would get some extra spending money out of the deal. Eric remembers thinking, "We probably waste that much money in office supplies every month, so what's the problem?"

"But it didn't take long to get past that and realize that this was not really about the money, it was about me and whether, in order to be a team player, I would cheat the company. I'm not naive. I'd heard about things like this in big companies, and of course I'd joined in the expense-account lunches. But this seemed very different. This meant lying and cheating and being compensated for it. The whole thing was just completely outside my value system, completely alien to how I'd been brought up."

But Eric didn't know what to do. He could turn in his expense report the way it was and simply refuse to change it or, hoping to avoid a confrontation, he could tell his boss that he didn't understand the image problem and would be more sensitive to it on his next trip and ask that the expense report be accepted as is.

In his dilemma he asked a couple of other young staff members for advice. They were almost dismissive of his ethical concern, and one warned him that he'd better just do what the department head wanted.

But he didn't. What he decided is that he would not turn in his expenses at all and would absorb the cost himself. When asked about it, he'd be honest and say what he'd done.

"It was not the most courageous decision," he says. "I didn't have the guts to just refuse to do what the boss said. I guess I just hoped the problem would go away."

Did it?

"No. He asked and I told him what I'd decided. He didn't get angry but said, 'I can't let you do that,' then said he'd take care of it."

The department head filled out an expense report for Eric, signed it, and submitted it, and a reimbursement check was issued to Eric.

"I cashed the check, kept what I was legitimately owed, and gave the rest to charity. I could have not cashed the check, but I knew that would probably just call more attention to the situation. So it probably was not the best solution, but it was the best I could come up with at the time."

After that, Eric admits he began staying in more expensive hotels and eating in more expensive restaurants. He at least wanted his reimbursements to be for legitimate expenditures even though he never felt completely comfortable spending more than was really necessary.

And he also began looking for another job.

LESSONS TO REMEMBER

- Find out all you can about the company culture before you take a new job.
- Be clear about your own values when confronted with a new situation.
- Be true to your values even when it means resisting a directive from the boss.

SEVEN

GO FOR THE NEXT BIG JOB OR
RETURN TO THE QUIET LIFE?

Every experience is important in making you
who you are.

WE LIKE TO beat up on our public servants in America, particularly the elected ones, except of course when we want something from them. Yet they have far more difficult and relentless demands on their attention than do executives of even the largest corporations. Elected officials' goals are by necessity broader and more complex, their constituencies are more unpredictable and difficult to satisfy, and their personal and family lives are often more at risk because the demands of the public always come first.

Some of our officials succeed admirably in balancing these often conflicting responsibilities; some don't. Those who do succeed, in order to accomplish anything, need four attributes: a thick skin, a strong work ethic, unflagging optimism, and an appreciation for the art of compromise.

Where are these attributes learned? The answer is probably different for different people, but for Governor Tom Vilsack of Iowa a major part of his learning began in his childhood home, an environment haunted by alcoholism and abuse.

Tom started life as an orphan. For the first years after his adoption, his home life was as normal as most children's. "Then, when I was roughly six or seven years of age, my mother began to drink quite heavily," he remembers. "There were initially periods of time when she would start drinking and then would stop for a period of a couple of weeks, then she would resume.

"Alcohol and drinking in our family was an accepted way of life. Both of my parents drank heavily, but my mother's situation got progressively worse. By the time I was about eight or nine years old, she would literally lock herself up in a part of our home for two or three weeks at a time. We wouldn't see much of her. There were even several times when she tried to commit suicide."

Then one day, she left. Over the years of her drinking, she had lied consistently, as many alcoholics do, about drinking. "She would tell me she wasn't drinking when she was. She would tell me she wouldn't drink again, then she would."

After several difficult years for the family, Tom's mother turned her life around, then she and his father got back together. By this time, Tom was a teenager. He was distrustful of his mother and he was angry, although he did what was expected of him, excelled in school, and went on to college and law school.

Years later, after he was elected governor, Tom visited family members in his hometown of Pittsburgh, Pennsylvania. One of them, also an alcoholic, showed him a letter his mother had written to her.

"She wrote about the last day she drank, the experience, the circumstances, what she was thinking, how she felt. I didn't know such a letter existed. In it she talked about how angry I was, yet I hadn't been aware that my anger was so transparent. As a kid, I had thought, 'They don't know how I really feel. I'm going to do what they expect me to do, be the son they expect me to be.' But my mother still knew I was angry."

Tom admits that he has always been very demanding of himself and, to a lesser extent, of others. He also says in the past he has not had the patience he should have had. But the letter changed all that for good. "I think it has impacted my relationship with everyone. I know I've become more understanding and more tolerant of different ways of thinking and doing things.

"I loved my mother a lot, and the older I get, the more I feel this profound respect for what she was able to do with her life. It was a dramatic and heroic thing. And I have started talking about the positive experiences I learned from her. She was a force in my life that taught me to never give up, and a force in my life that reminded me of the tremendous capacity of the human spirit. What she taught me is a very complex thing. I'm not sure I understand all of it, but it has to do with integrity within yourself, and it has to do with actions reflecting that integrity."

When Tom graduated from law school he married Christie Bell, the daughter and sister of lawyers in the town of Mount Pleasant, Iowa, where he and Christie settled into the quiet life of a small-town family. They had two sons, now both college graduates, and pursued the normal interests of middle-class Midwesterners: home, family, church, Little League, and school activities.

But that life took a dramatic turn when a disgruntled citizen walked into a city council meeting and shot and killed the mayor and a council member. The town went into shock. In what was to become the first in a series of hard choices about public service, Tom responded to the entreaties of the late mayor's father to seek the office and serve out the term.

Tom was elected, finished that term, and was elected again. During these years, he helped the town go through a period of healing, overcoming the shock of the murders. He worked to get housing built and to help reenergize the economy. By any measure, he was a successful mayor.

At the end of his second term, he chose not to run again. "I really think that change is part of the democratic calculation, and the system was not set up for professionals, for people to stay in these positions for a lifetime. Of course, if the voters want to reelect people, that's perfectly okay, but I felt it was time for me to get back to my family and my law practice full-time."

The people of Mount Pleasant had a different idea. Nobody ran for mayor, and the town was left with an open ballot. A group of citizens began a campaign to write in Tom's name, and he was elected again with a 97 percent write-in vote.

With encouragement from his family, all of whom were active in the political process in Iowa, Tom ran and was elected to the Iowa state senate about halfway through his third term as mayor.

In Iowa, the positions of senator and representative are basically part-time jobs in that they are paid only for the one hundred days that the legislature meets every year. This meant that, for the most part, Tom was still able to have a reasonably stable home life, coaching Little League, being with his sons Jess and Doug in their school years.

Then, in the spring of 1996, an Iowa congressman decided

to challenge one of the state's incumbent senators, "which meant," Tom recalls, "that there was going to be an open congressional seat. Everyone assumed that I was going to be the candidate for the Democrats because people felt I'd done a good job as a senator.

"You know, when you're in that situation and people are talking to you and encouraging you, you get flattered into thinking this is something you might want to do. So one day I announced to the press that I was going to tell them the next day what my decision was."

That evening, Tom went to his son Jess's final high-school basketball game, and Tom was swept with an overpowering realization of what a congressional seat would mean to his family. "I realized how much time I would spend away from them in Washington, D.C. I'd be flying back and forth, and I would miss some of Jess's life and a lot of Doug's life. I tell you, the feeling was enormous, to the point that I made the decision that not only was I not going to run for Congress but that I was done with public office."

It is difficult to say how much Tom's childhood experiences in a dysfunctional family intensified his commitment to maintain a stable, healthy environment for his own family, but those memories played a part in his decision not to seek a congressional seat and to leave public office.

Tom realized as he entered the statehouse on the day of his intended announcement that there was an atmosphere of high expectation among the press, his fellow legislators, and staff. News was about to be made.

Minutes before he was going to make the announcement, Tom told the senate majority leader his intentions. "I waited as long as possible to tell him because I knew people would try to talk me out of the decision."

The leader asked Tom not to specify the date of his leaving so that the party could manage the politics of a special election. Tom agreed to say only that sometime during the summer of 1996 he would leave his post.

Tom walked to his seat in the senate chamber and asked for an opportunity for a point of personal privilege. (This is a procedure by which the regular order of business is set aside briefly to allow an individual legislator to make a statement.) He rose and said, "I am not running for Congress. What's more, at the end of this session I'm leaving politics totally." He then left the chamber and went to his office to be alone.

The legislative session normally adjourns at the end of April, not to return until the following January. In May, Tom and the extended family gathered in Mount Pleasant to celebrate son Jess's graduation from high school. The plan was not only to honor Jess but to establish a scholarship at Iowa Wesleyan College in his grandfather's name.

"It was sort of a celebration of education," Tom says. "We had a wonderful dinner and made the presentation. Everyone was happy as a clam."

During the dinner, Christie's brother, Tom Bell, engaged Tom in a conversation that was to change Tom's life. "My brother-in-law was one of the most charismatic, energetic, wonderful people I've ever met in my life," recalls Tom, "so I always listened carefully to everything he said."

Bell was direct. "What are you doing?" he asked Tom. "You've done a good job. You have a gift for public service, you have a lot to offer, and there is much you could still do.

"I know you want to be there for your family," he continued, "but Tom, you have been. You only missed about two innings of Little League over all those years. You went to every basketball game. Listen, your kids are good kids. They love you. So what's the deal here?"

The next day Tom Bell died of a massive heart attack.

The conversation with Christie's brother and his subsequent death had a powerful emotional impact on Tom and turned out to be the turning point in leading him to make the hard choice to return to public service. If his beloved and respected brother-in-law felt this way, Tom reasoned, perhaps, based on his own childhood experiences, he had not given himself enough credit and had become his own worst critic. Perhaps he had projected onto his sons some of the needs he felt as a child and hadn't realized just how much he had been there for them.

"Tom Bell's death was the most shocking thing that's ever happened to me in my life. He was so full of life. There was just no reason for him to die at age fifty.

"It occurred to me that there was a point, a reason for that conversation. I think it challenged me, it suggested that I wasn't doing enough and needed to do more. This was a guy who gave 110 percent all the time. He gave everything he had, and now, all of a sudden, his spirit, his energy, his charisma, his desire for a better world was gone and it made me feel that somebody had to pick up the torch. I felt then that I had an obligation to stay in politics."

There's a lesson here about changing your mind: Don't be afraid to do it. Tom knew that he probably would catch some criticism in the press for changing his mind, but he also knew it was not the first time, nor would it be the last time, he'd be criticized for doing what he felt was right.

His family fully embraced the decision. In fact, it's fair to say that Christie and his sons had never felt that Tom should leave public service in the first place, but they had respected his decision and appreciated his reasons for making it.

Tom returned to the senate, where he served for two more years until, in 1998, he announced his candidacy for governor. He became the first Democrat elected governor of Iowa in thirty years. At this writing, he is in the final year of his second term and has won high marks not only for his leadership but for his ability to work with people in any situation, even those who vigorously disagree with him.

He explains that success partly as another lesson learned in childhood.

"I honestly don't hold grudges. I mean, I held this huge grudge against my mother for years and years. But now, it's like what's the sense of it?

"I've developed what some might consider an unusual practice. When someone really dislikes me, and I know it, I make an effort to sit down with that person and ask them, if they're willing, to explain their feelings to me and try to reach a point where there may not be affection between us but there is acceptance and respect."

Tom has done that many times in his life, even with people he's run against. "I've talked to people who weren't particularly nice when they ran against me. People in the senate have said some nasty things against me. I think I've won the respect of some of these folks by sitting down with them and saying, 'Let's talk about it.' "

Even with all his successes as governor, he has announced he will not seek a third term and, instead, is focusing intensely on finishing in the next year the initiatives begun in the past seven years. He has become active in helping people in other states run for governor.

Tom was one of the people on Senator Kerry's short list as

his vice presidential candidate in 2004, so naturally there is much speculation about Tom's future in public service.

Who knows at this point what his next hard choice will be? So far, if the governor knows, he's keeping it to himself. Whatever it is, there is no doubt that Tom Vilsack will continue to use the lessons he learned, often painfully, in childhood.

LESSONS TO REMEMBER

- Understand that every experience, even those from childhood, help make you who you are.
- Look for positive lessons, even from negative experiences.
- Be open to advice from those you trust.
- Don't be afraid to change your mind.

TAKE RESPONSIBILITY OR
RATIONALIZE YOUR MISTAKES?

*When you're in a major position, the easiest thing in
the world is to find someone else to take the heat.*

HOWARD BEHAR KEEPS two signs on his office wall. One
says, "Only the truth sounds like the truth." The other says,
"When you're in a hole, stop digging."

Howard admits that his beliefs about leadership and integrity are not those that have received a lot of publicity in recent years. "It seems that many business leaders feel they no
longer have to take responsibility for everything that happens in their business; they're only too glad to blame someone else. That's never been the way I've operated."

The press has been full of stories recently of CEOs whose
companies got into deep financial troubles but who claimed
to have no knowledge of the financial maneuvers that produced those troubles. Contrast those stories with how Howard
handled a financial crisis in his early days at Starbucks as vice
president for operations.

"I wanted to get our people above minimum wage at the
very beginning. And you know, it wasn't about a business

advantage. Everybody would say that the best thing to do is to try to lower your labor cost, but we were raising our labor costs intentionally because we felt it was the right thing to do."

So Howard did what any prudent executive would do. He had a financial analysis done on the impact of the wage increase. "I don't remember what the amount was, but it was significant. I said that we were going to raise starting wages and adjust the wages of everybody else. I think it was at least a dollar an hour, a very significant cost. But we'd done our research, and the analysis told us it was going to cost about one percent of sales, which, of course, is a lot. But we felt it was an investment worth making because we felt an investment in our employees was one of the best investments we could make."

So, with the support of Howard Schultz, founder of Starbucks and the man to whom Howard reported, they implemented the pay raise. And Howard went on vacation.

"Because I was on vacation, I didn't get to see the results of the first financial report. I remember getting this call from the analyst who'd done the work for me. He said, 'We made a mistake. The pay adjustment will cost us two and a half percent of sales, not one percent.' A huge difference and a huge problem."

He remembers Howard Schultz calling him. "He was a little peeved, as he should have been. So I said, 'It's my fault, I take full responsibility for the mistake.' "

Of course, the financial analyst had made the mistake. Shouldn't he have taken some of the responsibility?

"No," says Howard. "Of course he knew he'd made the mistake and he was shaken up by it, but I reviewed the data, I approved it. You know, you've got to step up and you've got to, what I affectionately call, take the bullet. It's never your people's responsibility. You may have a conversation later, you may reprimand them for the mistake, but it's always your responsibility first."

What about those CEOs who point at other people and say, often in court testimony, "Gee, I didn't know what was going on"?

Howard has a quick answer: "You get paid to know, and if you don't know you still get paid to know."

So he cut his vacation short, returned to work, enacted some cost-cutting and price-adjustment measures and was able to pay for the miscalculation in about sixty days. "We didn't even consider rolling back the wage increases," he says. "To have done so would have broken faith with our employees, plus it would have been doing the wrong thing instead of the right thing."

In addition to the wage policies, "Starbucks made a decision early on that we would offer health benefits and stock options to all as long as they worked more than twenty hours a week, and the majority did. Starbucks was probably the first large organization to ever provide its part-time workers with these benefits."

What were the advantages of taking on even more cost? "We were questioned about that," Howard says, "but at the time we had no idea whether it was going to serve any great business purpose, whether it was going to reduce turnover or help us attract better people, or any of that. We just made that decision because we felt that we all had to be in this together. I didn't feel I could walk down the hallway, look someone in the face, and say "We're all in this together" if that wasn't the truth. The CEO, the chairman, and the president shouldn't have any different health-care benefits than the part-time worker, because everyone gets sick equally."

Before his Starbucks days, Howard had a variety of business experiences, and he credits some of the early ones with teaching him the lessons of integrity by which he has tried to live his professional life as a manager and leader. A seminal experience occurred after he became president of a company that was in trouble.

"I really wanted that job," he recalls, "and I still have the letter I wrote to the CEO asking him to give me the opportunity to help. I didn't really have the education for the job, but I had the desire. When I got there, I knew what I had to do, I had to reduce costs. There was just no way out of it, and that meant we had to lay off some people.

"I'd never been through anything like that before; it was a totally new experience for me and quite painful."

So the decision was made and a layoff list was developed. Howard's plan was to meet with the people to be laid off, tell them of their options, the severance arrangements, and so forth. But something happened.

"The head of Human Resources had inadvertently left the layoff list on top of the copy machine. This was before computers, of course. I got the call next morning and the HR person told me what had happened. While I was trying to figure out how to respond, somebody, and I don't remember who, said something I've always remembered, 'Only the truth sounds like the truth.'

"So that morning I called a meeting of all the people working in the home office. And I laid it all out. I said, 'Here's what we have to do, and by the end of the day I promise that everybody will know where they stand.' "

This could have been a very toxic situation, with employees facing uncertainty about their very livelihood, but their response astonished Howard.

"I got a standing ovation," he says. "I was blown away. I thought they were going to be angry and hostile because the list got out and the situation seemed chaotic. But I discovered instead that if you give people the information, rather than treating them like children and giving them only the information you think they ought to have, you find that they can deal with the situation, however unpleasant it may be.

"The lesson to me is that if you are honest, if you act with integrity, even when it hurts, things will come out all right."

And Howard points out that this attitude goes for vendors as well as employees. "You have to ask how you treat the people who serve you well, both inside and outside of the company. Your values have to be your values all the time."

Howard recalls one example concerning a long-time supplier of Starbucks. "The supplier had served us fairly well since the early days of the company, but they were having some problems. It came to a point that some of the management team decided that the supplier no longer fit our needs. I remember sitting at a meeting where they presented their facts and conclusion.

"So I asked if they'd talked directly to the supplier. They gave sort of a half-hearted yes. Then I asked if they'd laid out the issues and tried to help them move along. Again a half-hearted yes. And I said, 'Don't you think it's important that that's where we go first? These people have been with us a long time. Even though I know you're having problems and you're not getting the things you want to get, you can't treat them any differently than you'd treat somebody working for the company.' And we had a long discussion after that."

On the surface it would not be a difficult choice to change vendors, regardless of the nature of the relationship. For many companies these days, balancing relationships and performance is not a hard choice. It always comes down to the numbers: If the numbers aren't right, the subject is closed. For these companies it would be unthinkable to invest management time and energy into helping a supplier become more effective for the company.

But Howard's feeling was that it was unacceptable to say, "Hey, we're going to get rid of these people and just let go after a ten-year relationship."

"A lot is involved," he says. "What about the effect on the people working for that supplier and what would have happened to them, not to mention the impact on our employees who had developed relationships with the supplier over the years."

Yet Howard refuses to blame his managers for what he felt was not a good decision. "I realized that I had not set the right tone. I had been pushing to improve results. I was saying things like, 'We've got to get better, we've got to have better products.' All those things. But sometimes you just can't go after results and forget about the effect that it has on people."

So did the supplier turn into an effective resource for Starbucks? Not in the long run. "Eventually, we did move away from that supplier," says Howard, "but they had the opportunity. We tried to improve them, and at the end of the day there were no surprises. Everybody knew what was expected and the decision became obvious for the supplier as well as for ourselves."

So if all this just meant postponing the inevitable, what was the point, what was the advantage?

"It's not just about the decisions you make, it's also about how you make the decision."

If anything seems to characterize Howard Behar's career

and his attitudes, it has been a willingness to make hard choices on behalf of his employees, the people closest to the customers, the processes, and the product.

When he started at Starbucks, he had the strong sense that this was a company that shared his values. "I really didn't need any proof," he says, "but when I'd been there only about three months I had an experience that told me everything I ever needed to know about the company."

The story began one day when a store manager said that he had something important he needed to discuss and asked to meet with both Howard Behar and Howard Schultz. Naturally, Howard asked if there was something he could do without meeting also with Schultz. "No," the manager said, "I need to talk to both of you."

So Howard set up a meeting.

"I remember Jim [the store manager] sitting down on the sofa and laying out his story. This was quite a few years ago, and he was the first person I'd known personally who had AIDS, although I didn't know it at the time. He simply said he was sick and dying."

The three sat quietly for several minutes.

"Then Howard Schultz began to cry," Howard recalls, "and I did too. Here was our founding father, who at the time was chairman, CEO, and president. He was all of it, you know, and after a few more minutes, the first words out of his mouth were, 'Jim, what can we do for you? You'll be here as long as you want to be here, and we'll cover all your insurance needs.' "

These words told Howard several things about the organization: "Number one, it was not about the company or about the founder, it was one hundred percent about Jim. Also I knew from that point on that I could make any decision to take care of people in the company and would always be supported."

There are all too few business executives who think this way because it requires a letting go of ego, an attitude of equal service to colleagues, employees, vendors, and customers, and it requires the courage to think long term rather than quarter to quarter, as well as a fundamental belief that the best interests of the company are always served by seeing to the best interests of its people.

Howard believes that some of the great challenges to integrity come in small doses. "The big things, you know, are fairly straight up," he says. "There's no one big answer to life, no one big answer to work, no one big answer to family. Everything you do counts, and it's a bunch of little things all along the way that put into motion the health of relationships.

"And with employees it starts with trust. They have to trust you, so right out of the gate you have to trust them first. You have to assume that everybody is trustworthy from the beginning. You don't wait for them to love you; you love them first."

This way of being represents a very hard choice for most managers, of course, because it requires time and energy. It means listening patiently and responding to the needs of everyone. But this, Howard insists, is the key to an ethical life as a manager and leader. "It means, as they say, walking the talk. I can't tell you how many times senior officers have left the company because they did not live the values, they only talked about them. It didn't make any difference to me what they earned, how many stock options they had, what their title or responsibilities were. If they couldn't help their people grow, if they didn't take care of their people, it was the quickest way out the door. This is what you have to do if you want integrity. You might have a great person running some division or some technical area, and they may have all the knowledge or creativity in the world about doing that, but if they can't take care of the people, they don't get to stay."

Some executives might assert that holding top people to this standard of behavior, regardless of what their other contributions may be, is not in the best interests of the business. It certainly is not the conventional wisdom.

But if you believe as Howard does that behavior that does not support the people is behavior that is not in the best interests of the business, then these are the hard choices you have to make, like it or not.

LESSONS TO REMEMBER

- Accept the fact that you get paid to know, and even if you don't know, you still get paid to know.
- Don't blame your people for things you're responsible for.
- Don't wait for your employees to trust you; trust them first.
- Understand that only the truth sounds like the truth.

NINE

BE A MANAGER OR BE A MINISTER?

How to deal with the things they don't teach in
seminary (or business school).

MANAGEMENT OF A nonprofit organization is a challenge in itself, but if the nonprofit also happens to be a church, the "manager's" problems multiply exponentially, and the hard choices take on a more highly charged moral dimension.

Think about the minister's roles. The job combines service, leadership, and organizational management. The minister is spiritual head of a congregation as well as chief executive officer of an organization, with responsibility for strategic planning leadership, budget development and oversight, and staff management.

Now think about this: The minister has to be visionary leader, spiritual counselor, teacher, and preacher for the very people who also are her boss, the people who hired her and can fire her.

One of the characteristics of nonprofit organizations is that alliances often develop between members of the paid staff and members of the volunteer board of directors, a very untidy situation in which directors are tempted to forget that their role is policy and, instead, involve themselves in operations and management. In so doing, they begin to second-guess the paid senior staff person. This is as true in a church as in any other nonprofit, but there's a further complicating factor; the staff are also members of the congregation, which means that they are part of the group who are, in effect, their boss's employers.

You probably could not find a more convoluted, complicated management situation than this. Yet the skills required of a minister/manager are not all that different from the ones required of any organizational leader. And the management situations a minister faces would be very familiar to any manager.

The Reverend Ms. Lynn Baker (not her real name) is minister of a mainline Protestant congregation and is also one of a handful of female senior ministers in her denomination. Lynn came to her present job over ten years ago. She had been senior minister of a smaller church in the Southwest and was recruited to lead the congregation of an older, well-established, and historically significant church in the Pacific Northwest. She is its first woman senior minister.

As in many organizations, the new leader can expect to be given reasonable freedom to build her own team. In preparation for Lynn's arrival in the job, the church's personnel committee had written a letter to all employees explaining that within six months Lynn would decide which staff members would remain in their jobs.

Lynn soon determined that one of her associate ministers, James, was not performing up to the requirements of the job. It became clear that other officers in the church, including members of the personnel committee, also had been concerned about James's performance. James did, however, still have strong support among some members of the congregation. Nonetheless, everyone felt that the new minister should make all staffing decisions.

Lynn admits there were times she wished the committee had just made the decision. "What was difficult for me," she says, "is that I knew I would have to make the choice and some people wouldn't like the choice. I felt everyone was watching and that how I handled this choice would signal how effectively I would work in the future."

Lynn's first step was to make the effort any good manager makes, to see if there was another job James could fill effectively, but as she investigated the possibilities, she concluded that his problems would be transferred to any other job.

"I knew this man was fearful of leaving the job, and the ethical question for me was, 'How do I help a person leave who doesn't want to leave more out of fear than out of a love of, and commitment to, the present job?' Was I going to help him leave and seek a future or was I simply going to be businesslike and let him go in an uncaring way?"

All managers inevitably face a situation like this at one time or another: an employee who has been with the organization for a while but who resists change, who has either not grown as the job has grown or who has become burned out or bored. Yet the person is too comfortable or too fearful to leave.

The management dilemma has two aspects: What's best for the organization, and what's best for the person? Whatever choice you make will create pain somewhere, either among the fellow workers who probably have to do a greater share of the work or with the deficient person. The deciding question always comes down to this: When am I so concerned about justice for the one person that I impose injustice on the group? You may try to avoid an unpleasant situation for yourself by either hoping the problem will go away on its own (it won't) or withdrawing your humanity from the situation and becoming the old top-down autocratic boss. Both approaches are tempting; neither works.

Even Lynn the minister was tempted by the institutional approach. "I could have said, 'I have a perfect right to let you go so I'm asking for your resignation,' but that would have been unfair to him, unfair to my ministry, and unfair to the congregation."

Because she was sensitive to the communal nature of a congregation and the personal connections involved, Lynn decided that she would handle the situation in full consultation with the officers of the church, explaining how she planned to handle it, what she planned to say. She was not seeking approval but wanted their understanding and support.

"I described to them what my dilemma was. I told them what I would do, that I wanted to help James come to a conclusion that was best for all."

Lynn's approach was first to ask whether or not James felt his ministry had concluded. Then next, Lynn described her expectations for anyone in this position and asked if he felt he could see a happy future for himself in that position. She also asked James to go to a counseling center, take some tests, and consult with the counselors.

"After that, he concluded that this was not the place for him."

Did Lynn pressure him?

"I did not," she insists. "I worked patiently with him to see that spiritually, emotionally, and in terms of his sense of service, this was probably not a place where he could begin again and experience wholeness in his sense of ministry."

But did he feel fired?

"I heard later that he did," Lynn says, "and I was sorry to hear it but not surprised. I probably would have felt the same way."

It's a fair question to ask if Lynn approached it the way she did as a thoughtful decision or because she didn't want to face the hard stuff of just saying, "Listen, this isn't working. You're fired."

"Absolutely not," she asserts. "I wanted to do it the way I did because that's what my ministry is about, that's what my life is about, paying attention. I mean, I'm a pastor. If I can't try to help this person make a healthy transition, what am I doing in this business?"

In a way, the best leaders embody aspects of the minister or counselor. They don't shy away from the hard decision of firing someone, but they also don't do it in a hard way. They understand that firing someone is basically a violent act, an attack on a person's sense of identity and self-worth, plus the taking away of a person's livelihood.

Even though these leaders know they will never be thanked by the person they've fired, they nonetheless do everything they can to support that person, both emotionally and materially. This approach of nurture, service, and compassion should be the norm in every such situation, unless of course the person was involved in illegal or unethical activities.

Lynn experienced from the episode with James a great deal of affirmation from the appreciative way the congregation and the church council responded. This clearly has enabled her to make other difficult changes and has even freed her in her teaching and preaching.

Yet there is never complete freedom in any leadership position. For a minister this often involves the message itself. Having to be the leader and the servant at the same time can be challenging, and even ministers have to learn how to draw the lines and make the choices.

"I think much of it has to do with authenticity and the willingness to be open and vulnerable. For instance, some people here think I'm too liberal and others think I'm not liberal enough. But in my evaluation I was greatly gratified to learn that people believed that when I spoke I was speaking from my own conviction and from my own sense of right and wrong. So that even when people in the congregation disagree with me, they can maintain a respect for me as a human being."

But Lynn admits there are subjects or situations she has been tempted to shade or compromise, or has chosen not to say things in a sermon she might have said.

"I'm often faced with those choices. Some I will compromise on, some I won't. For instance, I was not as strong about the war in Iraq as I might have been. I preached against it and I would like to have preached against it more strongly. But I have to be respectful of all the members of the congregation and I have members who supported the president's decision. So I was against the war and made that clear, but there is one's own sense of integrity about the war and the Christian mandates against it; then there's a sense of integrity that you have in serving the congregation. You just cannot scapegoat some of them. That also would not be in keeping with my Christian faith."

There are other areas of concern about which Lynn will not compromise regardless of congregation opinion. One is the rights of gay men and lesbians in their relationship with the church and with one another.

But aren't there members of the congregation who would be against gay rights and, if so, why is Lynn not "scapegoating" them by adamantly supporting those rights?

"This is a very different issue from war," Lynn insists. "While I made clear my opposition to the war, it is true that reasonable people disagree on that subject based on any number of circumstances. On the other hand, I believe that to deny rights to other human beings based on who they are as people is a clear and egregious violation of Christian teaching. The war was not something for which I would have sacrificed my job, but I would resign in a minute over my right and my need to minister to gay and lesbian people."

Including marriage?

"I have performed what we call 'covenant commitment ceremonies' for several years. I did them when I was in the East, I did them in the Southwest, and I've done them here. In fact, when I came here I knew I might be asked to do them. This church is an open and affirming congregation [meaning that membership and full participation are open to all people], so I went to the deacons and asked for a written policy that supports pastors in doing covenant commitment ceremonies. And they went right at it and got it done."

What if they hadn't, what if they had refused to have those ceremonies in the church?

"I would have resigned. There are a few principles that one cannot compromise. I was under care of the Presbyterian Church before I joined this denomination. I grew up in a fundamentalist church that doesn't ordain women, so I had to leave. Then, in 1979, the Presbyterians held their general assembly and said they wouldn't ordain gay and lesbian people, and while I personally am a happily married heterosexual, I left that denomination. This is a justice issue for which I will not compromise."

And what if no church would allow covenant commitment ceremonies?

"Well, that's not going to happen, but if it did, then I'd perform them outside the church. Listen, this is elemental. It's elemental in how we perceive the rights of human beings. I think that to be a human being, and particularly a human being of faith, means we can never choose to withhold the rights of other human beings whose only so-called transgression is to be who they are.

"I also consider that part of my essential role as leader of this congregation is to help people understand and embrace the moral and ethical choices we are called to make."

LESSONS TO REMEMBER

- Know where to draw the line between supporting and indulging.
- Take time to be a counselor when it's time for an employee to leave.
- Be clear about where you will and will not compromise.

HAVE COURAGE FOR A NOBLE CAUSE OR SURRENDER TO ANGER AND THREATS?

*When you get death threats, it would be easy to just
say, "To hell with it. I'm not making this decision."*

NOT MANY EXECUTIVES are stalked and receive death threats about a decision of integrity, but Robert Khayat experienced that and more when he was challenged to do the right thing in the face of enormous resistance. To understand what he was up against, you have to begin with a historical picture of the culture out of which the problems arose.

Not all that many years ago, when Robert starred on the University of Mississippi (Ole Miss) football team, the half-time show always began in the same way: A gigantic Confederate battle flag—the Rebel flag—unfurled from the end zone and began floating across the field to the tune of "Dixie." As the flag progressed, members of the Rebel Band "dropped out" from under and behind the flag to form the letter D, then I, then X, so that by the time the flag had finished its dramatic entrance across the field, the full band stood in formation spelling the word "Dixie." It was a spectacular beginning and it always put the crowd into a joyous frenzy.

It should be pointed out that the crowd was all white.

After graduating, earning a law degree, and subsequently serving as associate dean of the school of law, Robert Khayat was tapped to become the fifteenth chancellor of the university. By this time, Ole Miss was integrated, with ever more African-American students attending yearly. To no one's surprise, the African-American students, plus many of their white colleagues, were not enamored of the Rebel flag as the symbol of their university, and they didn't care much either for hearing Dixie played after every touchdown.

But there were thousands of alumni as well as perhaps half of the student body who felt that the flag and the song had lost their racist symbolism and were merely elements of the overall school spirit. To them, these symbols were considered sacrosanct and they were not to be messed with. Period.

Thus, in the final decade of the twentieth century, things were changing. On the one hand, there was the obvious progress represented by racial integration of the university. On the other, there were issues about attitude and belief, tradition and symbolism. What was an appropriately reverent respect for Ole Miss history and its symbols versus the sensitivities of those offended and hurt by racist displays? And who should resolve these conflicts?

The overriding question for Robert Khayat concerned the possible effect all this might be having on public perceptions of the university.

"When I took this job in 1995, I really started looking at where we were," says Robert. "We had lost one thousand students between '91 and '95. Our enrollment had declined seven percent. Our costs had increased twenty-nine percent. We were headed for a train wreck."

Robert needed to know why, so he told his management team that he wanted some kind of assessment that "will tell us why people are not coming to school here." He called for an image study, to find out how the university was perceived by the general public.

As the university's faculty and students began to hear about the assessment plan, a reporter from the student newspaper, the *Daily Mississippian*, visited Robert. He told her about the image study and why he felt it needed to be done.

"So," she asked him, "are you going to deal with the symbols, the flag, the song, Colonel Rebel [a caricature of a plantation "colonel"], the Confederate statue?"

"Of course," Robert answered. "We're going to deal with the symbols because we're going to deal with everything that affects the way people view us."

The next day's newspaper headline read "Ole Miss to Review Symbols."

"Well," Robert says, "I got an education. I had no idea about the emotional investment that people make in symbols. I confess I just didn't appreciate it."

The article led to more specific questions about what would be reviewed. Robert's answer was the same: "Everything that affects the way people perceive us, from the academic programs to the faculty to the library to the beauty of the campus, and yes the flag and all the symbols.

"As for the flag, we're going to have to deal with it because it has been appropriated by people with whom we do not want to be associated. First of all, it's not an official symbol of the university, and secondly, it does not represent the university well."

Once the specific items for examination appeared in the regional press, the explosion began and, in Robert's words, "I knew I had stepped on a land mine and I really wasn't competent to deal with it. I needed professional help."

The flag became the biggest and most visible issue. Robert discussed it with a generous alumnus who made it clear that he also felt the flag had to go and who made a major financial contribution to the effort so that Robert could engage a national public relations firm (the senior partner of which was also an Ole Miss alumnus) to help sort out the issues and work through a process.

"We had press conferences and gave students and other groups a chance to talk to us. We listened to everyone and worked our way through it over about a nine-month period."

During all this, Robert became the target of anger and hostility. "People quit speaking to me. Guys I played football with, and coaches, and alums. And there were crazy people who wanted to kill me, some of whom even lived in other states. That sort of thing."

Robert received about fifteen death threats. He turned those over to the FBI and the U.S. attorney's office but chose not to add security or hire a bodyguard. He later learned he had also been stalked by a man who, it turned out, was being watched for other reasons by the state highway patrol.

Did he fear for the safety of his family? "Not my family," he says, "but I was afraid something was going to happen to the students. One time a guy came in, you know, a militia type. He had on combat fatigues and boots and was carrying a Confederate battle flag that was about eight by twelve feet. About thirty to forty-five kids gathered around him and he starting railing about seceding from the nation. For the most part the kids just got to laughing, but you never know if someone's going to pick up a rock then, boom, all of a sudden you've got a fight on your hands. I tell you, we were really on edge during that whole time."

Early in the controversy, there began to appear in the football stadium, during the games, thousands of small Rebel flags. A correspondent from the *New York Times* Atlanta office photographed the stadium with all the flags and did an article on the situation. Suddenly, Ole Miss was in the national news, and it was not helpful.

Even with the publicity and the apparent unhappiness of some, the decision about the flag had been made, and it had been made properly. There comes a time in most organizations when the people involved will be divided about the right thing to do. This is the true test of a leader's skills because the old way of top-down decision-making simply will not work. What's required is a process of consensus-building in which the people who matter most can participate in the decision and help find useful and productive ways to make it work in the organization's best long-term interest. Also understand that this process will not make everybody happy, but there comes a time when the appropriate objective is to build the consensus, implement the decision, and then work to nurture support from those who disagree.

In a company, the people who matter most are the owners, employees, and customers, and depending on the decision, the vendors and community in which the company operates. For Robert, those people were the students, alumni, administration, and public officials and community leaders. It was those people who were brought into the process and whose opinions and ideas were given full consideration before the final decision was made. Without that process of consensus-building and careful communication with everyone involved, it is doubtful that Robert would have been able to achieve the final positive result.

But sometimes, even after the right process and the right decision, and the attempts to reach out to those who disagree, you can still face resistance. In Robert's case, what was to be done about all those flags at football games? It was not possible to ban individual citizens from bringing a flag to a football game.

Robert's solution was elegant and simple: "The key to our success was that, for safety reasons, we agreed to ban sticks in the stadium. That's how we did it. We wouldn't allow anything that had any pointed object. No umbrellas, no hot dogs on a stick, nothing."

Were there diehard reactions? "Of course, but they couldn't wave a flag; they could wave a limp rag if they wanted to. Some of them wore Confederate T-shirts, but that pretty much just went away."

Robert does not take the hero's role in all this. "The real heroes were the students and our alums."

The student government supported Robert's decision, as did the *Daily Mississippian*, and "we got the unanimous support of all ninety of the Alumni Association Board of Directors even though there were alums who were against the decision and who threatened to withhold financial support.

"And on game day, if someone came onto the campus with a Rebel flag or staged some kind of demonstration, our alumni would quell it. They'd gather around and say things like, 'You must not be an Ole Miss person because we don't behave this way.'"

One of the things that gave Robert satisfaction and a sense of poetic justice was a follow-up visit by the *New York Times*

Atlanta correspondent, who the previous year had published a photograph of the flags in the stadium and written a big story about the conflict. "This time he could not find one flag in the stadium. He took a picture of that, and the *Times* ran photos of both situations. This time, his article was very complimentary."

Robert is extravagant in his praise of the Ole Miss community. "I'm not inflating this when I say the students and the staff were really courageous. Our management team, the vice-chancellors held firm. The alumni association, the foundation board, student senate, faculty senate, all those groups that could have a resolution, passed one supporting our position."

But Robert admits that somebody has to lead and that it wasn't always an easy position to hold. "I know it was the right thing to do, but I will tell you there were times during those nine months I had trouble sticking with it. Some days I'd say, 'Well, just the hell with it, let them have the flag, but I'm thankful I never gave in to those negative thoughts because the positive changes have been enormous."

One of the most significant academically was, within two years of the flag episode, Phi Beta Kappa awarded a charter to the university. "And they told me directly that we would not have gotten that charter had the flag issue not been dealt with."

So what about "Dixie"?

"We still play 'Dixie,' " Robert says, "but we play a very different version of it. It's called 'From Dixie with Love,' and it's half 'Dixie' and half 'Battle Hymn of the Republic.' It's actually a beautiful song. It starts off with the slow 'Dixie' and the slow 'Battle Hymn,' then it kicks in and becomes a pep song. It's an old Elvis song and it seems to please everyone. Isn't that amazing?"

Now, ten years later, was the struggle worth it?

"Absolutely," says Robert. "Not only has it been personally satisfying, but to quantify it, contributions are up, enrollment is up, our African-American student enrollment is up thirteen percent this year, and we're becoming what an American, and a Southern, university should be. We had two student body presidents who were black, two *Daily Mississippian* editors who were black, an African-American Miss Ole Miss, and this year, two black students inducted into the Hall of Fame."

Again, Robert refuses to take the credit but shares it with his management team, his faculty, and the students. "Listen," he says, "I have all sorts of failings and I make mistakes every day, but I try my darnedest not to embarrass the university, my family, or myself. This job is different from the private sector, where you have to hit the bottom line and make those shareholders happy. We have a broader constituency, and I think there are more opportunities to make the wrong choice."

Robert says he has faced many challenging situations and continues to do so, though none as dramatic as the flag episode. "As for the flag situation, it was a matter of whether I had the courage to do it, then whether, with people just trying to wear me out, I could summon up the staying power."

LESSONS TO REMEMBER

- Build consensus when starting to make a major cultural change.
- Never underestimate the importance of symbols.
- Be creative and innovative in accomplishing your goals.
- Don't be intimidated by threats.

ELEVEN

TELL THE PUBLIC EVERYTHING OR SUPPRESS THE NEWS?

How do you stand up to your colleagues, peers, and almost everyone else in your business?

MICHAEL GARTNER IS a third-generation Iowa newspaperman who believes, with all his heart, in two things: the First Amendment and fairness.

That wouldn't seem very controversial.

But his beliefs were tested—and criticized and assailed—in 1991, when a woman said she was raped by William Kennedy Smith, a nephew of President John Kennedy. At the time, Michael was in the middle of a five-year stint as president of NBC News, halfway through reshaping the network's news division financially and journalistically. He spent most of his time on financial, organizational, policy, and strategic matters, but he also kept a close eye on content.

Networks had rarely had to think about the issues in covering allegations of rape, for those stories rarely had risen to the level of national news. But Michael had thought about the issue for years as the editor of a regional newspaper—the *Des Moines Register*—in which charges of rape regularly made the news. Ultimately, Michael concluded that the press should name the accusers as well as the accused. That became his newspaper's policy.

His reasoning was clear. "I could argue the case on socio-logical grounds," he says. "I could point out that rape is a crime of violence, not of sex. That women who are raped—and their friends and their families and society as a whole—should be outraged by the crime. That the women themselves should feel fury, not shame. I could argue that the press's re-fusal to name accusers added to a conspiracy of silence that reinforced the stigma of rape and that that stigma would remain with the victims, or alleged victims, until the press started dealing with the crime the way it dealt with murder and mayhem—by naming names and eliminating secrecy. I could draw parallels to the days when it was deemed shame-ful if someone in your family had cancer—in those days, those people died 'of a long illness,' never of cancer. I could draw parallels to the early days of AIDS, when no one would talk about the disease—and there was thus little education about it and little research into it."

But, he continues, "I'm a journalist, not a sociologist or a criminologist or a health researcher. To me, it boiled down to a simple journalistic issue of fairness."

In a story on crime, he explains, if you name the person who is accused, you simply must name the accuser as well. Otherwise, you're withholding a key fact from the reader, you're putting out a story that is unbalanced, and, however many times you use the word "alleged," you're still letting an anonymous person label a named person as a rapist. "That's just unfair," Michael says. He saw two solutions: Name the accuser, or quit naming the accused.

The second solution was impractical and flawed. It meant

doubly withholding information—two wrongs, in Michael's view. So he settled on the first solution, naming names unless either party was a juvenile. "We were in the business of disseminating news, not suppressing it," he says.

He watched with more-than-casual interest as the William Kennedy Smith story became a national story. At first, NBC, like its counterparts, didn't name the woman. That privately troubled Michael. So one day, as the story continued, he went to the morning news meeting at NBC and raised the issue. If the story is not going to go away, he said, "let's discuss whether we should name the woman."

There were probably thirty to forty people in the room that morning, he recalls, and there was a robust discussion. Many people had never thought about the issue. Most assumed, in fact, that it wasn't an issue—that NBC, like all the mainstream national media, simply would not name her. The meeting lasted longer than usual. At the end, Michael stated his case. One of the questions he asked: What if Smith didn't do it, what if he is acquitted? Will we add to his stigma—going through life as a "rapist" when he isn't one, wrongly accused by a nameless woman?

"I didn't ask for a vote—newsrooms aren't democracies," Michael recalls now, more than a decade later, "but it was clear to me that only a handful of people in the room wanted to name the woman."

The handful included Michael. So that evening, *NBC Nightly News* matter-of-factly noted that the name of the woman who was accusing William Kennedy Smith of rape was Patricia Bowman.

An hour or so before the show was to air, Michael sent a notice to the network's two-hundred-plus affiliates telling them of his decision. A half-dozen complained. At least one, in Boston, bleeped out the woman's name and covered her picture. Most said nothing directly to Michael, though they talked about it incessantly among themselves and with other NBC executives.

The next day, the *New York Times* also named Ms. Bowman.

Michael's decision rekindled a debate in journalistic, feminist, and legal circles. He was widely and loudly assailed by many social workers, feminist activists, and prosecutors who said the naming of victims was a cruel second blow to women who had been raped. They said Gartner was an unprincipled man, a man putting sensation above compassion, a man with no heart and no conscience.

"What if it had been your wife or your daughter?" he was repeatedly asked. First, he replied, I'd try to strangle the man. Second, he said, I would hope that my wife or my daughter would feel fury, not shame. And third, he said, I would name them in the paper, hoping that it would ultimately lead to a better understanding of the crime, to more women coming forth to report the crime, and to harsher penalties for the crime. That proved, his critics said, how heartless he was.

"I don't recall anyone ever publicly taking the position that my view was a principled journalistic view, that fairness should be a journalistic tenet in every story even when fairness led to discomfort, or that—and this was never noticed—we went through a thorough journalistic process in debating the issue," Michael recalls. "No one said they admired my integrity," he says. "Well, my wife might have said that. But I'm not even sure about that."

As he watched the show that night, Michael worried that he might have jeopardized the all-important ratings of *Nightly News*—which some NBC marketing people feared—but he also says he could have lived with a hit to the ratings more easily than he could have lived with a hit to his principles. As it turned out, the ratings weren't affected, and neither were his principles.

Within the news division itself, there was much discussion but little dismay. Part of that was because of the process Michael went through. He is a big believer in process. He says that, first, he discussed the issue privately with key people on his staff and top NBC people outside the news division. Then he had a thorough and open discussion with all the people involved. Then he told anyone involved in the story that he or she could opt out if they disagreed with the decision. Finally, he sent a long memo to the staff explaining the decision. "Process is everything," Michael says. "It's especially important during times of stress or controversy."

One other thing made him feel good. A week or two after the airing, he said, two women from NBC came to his office separately and said they wanted to talk. "Each had been in that morning news meeting. Neither had said much. Each told me that she was glad NBC had aired the name. Each said she believed it would lead to a wider understanding of rape, to an easing of the stigma. Then each said she had been raped. And each said she had never reported it. Each told me the discussion in the news meeting was painful but important, and each thanked me."

Few people remember the William Kennedy Smith story today. He was acquitted—and, Michael notes amazingly, "even then most newspapers did not name Ms. Bowman." In fact, she continued to refer to herself as a rape "victim" in national appearances and assailed "media organizations" for naming her "without my consent . . . simply because I was a victim of crime." And, again ignoring the court decision, she added, "The rape destroyed me." At Stanford, in 1992, she got a standing ovation after giving a talk entitled "Surviving the Media: A Victim's Perspective."

Michael left NBC in 1993 and went back to Iowa, where he won a Pulitzer Prize for writing editorials—many about the First Amendment—for a small newspaper he owned and where he bought a Triple-A baseball team and promptly hung a copy of the First Amendment prominently in the concourse. "If people are going to yell 'Kill the umpire!' " he says, "they should know where they get that right."

He was long gone from NBC and from journalism in 2004 when a case similar to the Smith case arose. Kobe Bryant, the Los Angeles basketball star, was accused of raping a woman at a resort in Colorado. It was a huge story, bigger than the William Kennedy Smith story. It was on all the networks, in all the newspapers.

"I watched and read carefully," Michael says, "to see if times had changed, to see if networks and newspapers would routinely name the woman." None, including NBC, did.

Ultimately, the charges were dropped. Still, no network or mainstream newspaper named the woman.

Then she sued Bryant in civil court.

And no one named her even then.

"Clearly," Michael observes about the Bryant events, "not much has changed. In fact, it looks like the press has gone backwards on the issue."

Does that bother him? "Not really. One of the great things about a free press is that no one dictates what is right and what is wrong. I know what I think is right and what I think is wrong, but others have other views. That's what makes democracy. The main thing is this: Despite the consequences, real or imagined, you must remain true to your beliefs."

That goes for journalism or baseball or parenting or anything else, he says.

"I got beaten up pretty badly," he recalls about the Smith-Bowman case. "But it didn't hurt. I didn't compromise my beliefs. If I had, that's what would have hurt."

Below is the memo Michael sent to his staff:

To the staff:

Why did NBC News name the woman who says she was raped at the Kennedy compound in Florida over the Easter weekend? How was that decision made?

For years, the issue has been debated by journalists and feminists: should the names of rape victims or alleged rape victims be made public? Among journalists, there is no agreement; among feminists, there is no agreement. At NBC, we debated the journalistic arguments.

Some background: I have been deeply interested in this subject for years, discussing it and debating it. Years ago, I concluded that journalistically, it is usually right to name rape victims. Usually, but not always. Here is my reasoning.

First, we are in the business of disseminating news, not suppressing it. Names and facts are news. They add credibility, they round out the story, they give the viewer or reader information he or she needs to understand issues, to make up his or her own mind about what's going on. So my prejudice is always toward telling the viewer all the germane facts that we know.

Second, producers and editors and news directors should make editorial decisions; editorial decisions should not be made in courtrooms, or legislatures, or briefing rooms—or by persons involved in the news. That is why I oppose military censorship, legislative mandate, and the general belief that we should only print the names of rape victims who volunteer their names. In no other category of news do we give the newsmaker the option of being named. Those are decisions that should be made in newsrooms—one way or another.

Third, by not naming rape victims we are part of a conspiracy of silence, and that silence is bad for viewers and readers. It reinforces the idea that somehow there is something shameful about being raped. Rape is a crime of violence, a horrible crime of violence. Rapists are horrible people; rape victims are not. One role of the press is to inform, and one way of informing is to destroy incorrect impressions and stereotypes.

Fourth, and finally, there is an issue of fairness. I heard no debate in our newsroom and heard of no debate in other newsrooms on whether we should name the suspect, William Smith. He has not been charged with anything. Yet we dragged his name and his reputation into this without thought, without regard to what might happen to him should he not be guilty—indeed, should he not even be charged. Rapists are vile human beings; but a suspect isn't necessarily a rapist. Were we fair? Probably, yes, because he was thrust into the news, rightly or wrongly. But so was Patricia Bowman, and we should treat her the same way journalistically. We are reporters; we don't take sides, we don't pass judgment.

Those are the points made in our internal debates. At NBC News, I first raised the issue when the woman was raped in Central Park. We had one story on *Nightly*

News, and after that I told some colleagues that if that were to become a continuing national story we should debate the question of naming the woman. As it turned out, it did not become a continuing national story, and we did not have the debate at that time.

Two weeks ago, I began debating in my own mind the issue of the Florida case. I joined in the debate with some colleagues from outside NBC News last week. On Monday of this week, I raised the issue with three colleagues within NBC News. We discussed it at some length. Should we do this, and if we did it how should we frame it?

On Tuesday, the discussions continued. They were passionate and spirited, but not mean-spirited. By the end of the day, the debate probably encompassed thirty persons, men and women of all views. There was no unanimity; if a vote had been taken, it probably would have not been to print the name. But I decided for the reasons listed here, to air the name. The fact that her identity was known to many in her community was another factor—but not a controlling one—in my decision. There were those—including some involved in the preparation, production, and presentation of the piece—who disagreed intellectually. But no one asked to be removed from the story, and everyone did a thorough job. The story was clear and fair and accurate; it was not sensational, and—for those who think it was done for ratings or the like—it was not hyped or promoted. It was presented as just another very interesting story in a *Nightly News* broadcast that, that night, was full of especially compelling stories.

At 5:00 P.M., we did send an advisory to affiliates that

we were naming the woman, for our Florida affiliates, especially, needed to be told in advance. In the time since, six of our 209 affiliates have complained to us about the decision; at least one, WBZ in Boston, bleeped out the woman's name and covered her picture. Several affiliates said we ran counter to their own policies, but just as we respect their views they respected ours and ran the story. Several other affiliates called to say they agreed with our decision. Most said nothing.

I am particularly proud of the process we went through in reaching our conclusion; in fact, the process was more important than the conclusion. There was vigorous and free debate about an issue of journalism; all sides were discussed. The story was shaped and re-shaped as a result of that debate. When we ultimately decided to air the name, everyone involved at least understood the reasons, and everyone then did the usual first-rate work.

Our decision engendered a national debate. Much of the debate has been focused on the wrong issues, but much of it has been focused on the right issue: the crime of rape. The debate itself has raised the awareness of the horribleness of the crime, the innocence of victims, the vileness of rapists. That has been a beneficial side effect.

Rape is rarely a national story. If another rape becomes a big story, we will have the same debate again. The position at NBC News is this: we will consider the naming of rape victims or alleged rape victims on a case-by-case basis.

Gartner

LESSONS TO REMEMBER

- Seek advice and counsel in the face of difficult decisions.
- Realize that process is important in times of stress and controversy.
- Be open with information and intentions.

INTERVENE ON BEHALF OF THE EMPLOYEES OR TOLERATE AN EXECUTIVE BULLY?

*When you try to do the right thing, damned if
sometimes it just doesn't turn out wrong.*

AT ONE TIME or another, every manager will face this situation: An employee or group of employees asks for a meeting, then in the meeting also asks that the meeting be kept confidential. Further, they want assurances that their names will not be revealed as sources of the information they are about to report.

This is a no-win situation for the manager. In those circumstances, just what is he or she expected to do? The employees want action of some sort, but how does the manager take action and still maintain the confidences?

The authors suggest that the manager state right up front that "If you want me to keep all this in confidence, then my hands are tied. I'd be happy to listen and comment if you wish, but if you want me to do something to resolve the situation, chances are I can't keep this meeting or your names confidential. I'll try, but I can't guarantee it. Fair enough?"

Sometimes, of course, what the manager learns in the

meeting may be so troubling that action is required, even if there is a risk of inadvertently betraying confidences.

This is the situation that Daniel Thomas (not his real name) faced several years ago. He took action, and he felt he did the right thing, but the outcome has haunted him ever since. It has also moved him to resolve that he will always ensure that employees who put their trust in him will never regret it. "Never again," he emphasizes. "I'll put my job on the line first."

As the chief administrative officer of a large international company, Daniel often found himself in the position of counseling employees, resolving conflict between people and groups, and intervening in ethically and legally inappropriate situations. It just went with his territory, and he was successful in navigating the often-intense ego clashes that frequently characterize the workplaces of highly creative people.

One day, he was approached by a group of employees who asked for a confidential meeting. He agreed. The employees presented a solid front and stated a compelling case against their manager. She behaved, they said, beyond any reasonable definition of professionalism. She ranted, she screamed, she belittled and ridiculed them, she threatened their jobs, and she treated them as less than human. Her behavior, they insisted, was beyond abusive, it was bizarre.

Not only their words but also their body language in the meeting convinced Daniel that these employees were scared to death of the manager and scared of retribution if she found out they had come to him. "They literally begged me," Daniel says, "to keep their names out of this, so I assured them that I would do my best to maintain their confidence."

Daniel's next step was to do his own due diligence, to determine if what the employees alleged was true or was an exaggeration of simple hard-nosed management behavior. "We investigated it seriously for about a month, during which time we never blew the employees' cover. One of my HR directors, responsible for day-to-day HR for that division, told me there had been rumblings about this problem for quite a while. What we discovered is that it was absolutely true. We found that the manager was abusive, vindictive, and bullying."

Daniel's analysis was that the manager, who was in a key position overseeing a very successful product, was under enormous pressure to keep the product performing. He felt she was out of balance, that she needed some professional help, and that it was the company's responsibility to help her.

It should be understood that the manager was not in a reporting relationship to Daniel as chief administrative officer. His was a staff role, though a very substantial one.

So he developed a plan and presented it to his boss, the CEO of the company. It was, Daniel felt, a plan that was both generous to the manager and responsive to the employees: He would suspend her with pay for thirty days and offer outside services, specifically psychotherapy, during this period. The CEO told him to do what he thought was right but first to work it out with the manager's boss, the president of the division. This is where the relationships get tricky.

First, the manager was a close friend of her boss, the division president. Next, the manager was married to another company executive who happened to be the brightest and fastest rising star in the division. While the president might have been willing to risk losing her friend the manager, she was not willing to lose the husband.

Daniel explained the situation to the president of the divi-

THE BOOK OF HARD CHOICES

sion, telling her that he was going to do what amounted to an intervention, as might be done with someone with a substance abuse problem, suspend her, and urge her to seek help at the company's expense.

"I absolutely disagree with what you want to do," the president said to Daniel. "This is going to make big problems for us; we can't afford for her husband to leave, and he is going to be very angry." The president's suggestion was that the manager be disciplined and told to shape up, or words to that effect, plus perhaps get some therapy, but not to be put on leave. Her attitude seemed to be that Daniel should just tell the manager to fix the problem and let it go at that.

"Look," Daniel replied, "I'm not suggesting that we fire her. Everyone feels her work is good and that she's producing a beautiful product. But it won't work to discipline her and tell her, in effect, to 'fix the problem,' because this is not normal behavior. Her people are petrified that if she is not required to stay away from the office, the retribution against them will be like a holocaust."

But the president's concern was only with her key managers, not with the people, so she told Daniel, "Okay, do what you think is necessary, but I don't agree with you, and it's on your head."

Daniel and the president were peers in the company, and while Daniel's responsibilities as CAO clearly empowered him to act in this situation, the direct reporting relationship was between the manager and the president. Daniel did not want to offend the president and create an uncomfortable working relationship with his peer; he did not want to so anger the manager that she would walk out, taking her husband with her; and he did not want to intensify the hostile working environment for the employees. Add these concerns to his sincere intention to help the manager, to improve her personal and professional life.

So he called her in, took her through the problem, outlined the process of a thirty-day suspension with pay, and offered the company's support in providing outside services if she wanted to take advantage of them. He urged her to do so. "We'll never know what's said," he told her. "And we'll never have any idea about anything other than you're attending the sessions."

Then the meeting became emotionally difficult. "She broke down," Daniel says, "and, you know, it was very emotional for both of us. She said her employees didn't understand her or the pressure she was under. She was worried that this action would ruin her reputation. But I stuck to my guns and emphasized that we were going to do whatever we could to help her, and that if she elected to do the therapy, this in itself might help relieve some of the pressure she felt. I told her, however, that she had to take the suspension and she was not to come into the office during this time."

After the meeting, with the manager on her way home, Daniel took his next step, which was to meet with her husband. He felt he owed the husband an explanation directly. "I tried to explain to him that we were trying to help, but I told him that the situation was serious enough that we had no choice. I told him I hoped he would support the suggestion about counseling."

The husband's reaction?

Daniel found him appropriately defensive of his wife. In addition, "he was surly and uncommunicative with me, but he listened and thanked me for informing him."

The manager went through the psychotherapy, as suggested, but she did not stay away from the office. In fact, she went into the office when she didn't think anyone would know and, Daniel has always suspected, her husband covered for her.

"We had tried to deal with her in a grown-up way," Daniel says. "We didn't take her building pass or her keys or anything like that. We treated her with respect and assumed that she would not violate this honor system. But she did.

"And her mission was clear. She intended to discover the names of the people who had come to me. And she did. I don't know who helped her, but the damage was done."

Daniel felt her behavior was reprehensible. "I went to the division president and said, 'Because of her behavior and her violation of our trust, I don't think we can bring her back to work with these people. She has identified them, and she is not a mature enough person to be able to deal with this professionally. She won't look to find a remedy, she'll look to wreak vengeance.'"

He recommended she be fired. The division head made clear that she would veto the recommendation. "I gave you your thirty days," she told Daniel. "She's got to come back; I can't lose her husband." The division head then appealed directly to the CEO.

Daniel had serious misgivings about the solution the president proposed: that the manager return to work but be kept on probation and be asked to voluntarily continue the therapy.

Before he could try to make the case against that plan, Daniel received a substantial and highly desirable promotion to another division of the company. Any manager knows that these kinds of opportunities are rare and that to refuse such a promotion not only disrupts the plans of the company but also probably diminishes future opportunities. Daniel felt compelled to accept the promotion, but he was torn. He realized that this would necessarily remove him from any involvement in the continuing situation with the offending manager.

"In the period after I moved to the other job," Daniel explains, "she fired or forced out every one of those people to whom I'd given my word. It was the only time in my career that I was not able to keep my word to people who trusted and counted on me. Ethically and morally, I knew the right thing to do, but I was not supported in that and was no longer in a position to intervene in any way."

The violation of confidence and the subsequent vengeance exacted against the people have weighed heavily on Daniel for several years. "I thought the right thing would be done by the organization," he says, "that the employees would be protected even if we ultimately couldn't protect their identity. And for me it is entirely personal; they trusted me and they trusted my integrity and they trusted their knowledge of who I was as an executive and as a man."

The aftermath was painful, and Daniel still is haunted by the memory of it. "I can remember, clear as day, one young woman who had been an office assistant for a number of years. When it was all over and she was leaving, she came to my new office and said, 'It wasn't your fault. You did what you could.' And you know, it was the most gracious thing for this young woman to do. I've never felt I deserved her forgiveness."

This episode has led Daniel to a solid commitment that he will never let this happen again. "I am never going to allow employees to regret putting their trust in me. Never again. I am resolved to be much more aggressive in the future, even to the point of putting my job on the line."

There are other lessons Daniel has drawn from this experience. One is that whenever he is asked to keep a confidence, he'll say, "If you ask me to keep this in confidence, I can as long as no one else is in jeopardy, no crime is being committed, there's no threat of physical harm, or it's not an issue of sexual harassment. If it's anything else, I'll keep it confidential as long as I can.

"I also say that I can advise you, I can counsel you, but I can't fix the problem for you and I can't help you fix the problem because you're not authorizing me to go to whatever the source of the problem is and research it. If you want me to help you, then we have to adjust exactly what it means to keep the confidence."

So the sad result of Daniel's hard choice to try to protect employees while solving the management problem has resulted in a more clearly defined ethical framework for confronting these issues in the future. It's a lesson that can easily be applied to a wide variety of organizations.

LESSONS TO REMEMBER

- Set clear ground rules before making any commitment to confidentiality.
- Understand that doing the right thing sometimes turns out wrong.
- Process and review whatever actions you take so that you can do them better next time.

THIRTEEN

QUIT YOUR JOB OR SUPPORT A LIE?

So they give you this big job, then they expect you to
support numbers you know are wrong. So?

THE TERM "WHISTLEBLOWER" has taken on such mixed connotations that perhaps it's time to put the word to rest. The person labeled a whistleblower is often viewed negatively by people in business, government, and the military, not to mention the church. This is an attitude as old as organizational life itself: Blame the messenger.

It may be true that some people who blow the whistle on certain practices are motivated by revenge, but the record seems clear that most of the time these are people who just can no longer support activities that are in conflict with their values. In other words, more often than not, those who expose the unwelcome truth are acting from an imperative of personal integrity.

Sometimes they can't get satisfaction within the organization itself and have to "go public." Often, however, they are able to find relief and support from higher-ups who recognize that the situation has to be dealt with forthrightly. Even so, the people who expose the unethical or illegal activities rarely feel that their actions have been fully appreciated, and there is often an emotional price to pay, even when things turn out okay.

This is the story of Doris Mitchell (not her real name). She was a star. There's no other way to put it.

She began her career as an attorney. She built a successful practice and could have continued to prosper as an attorney for the rest of her career. But her interests and ambitions were broader than the law itself.

"I was very happy practicing law, but I really wanted to get into the business side of things."

The opportunity came; not only that, it was a big opportunity. She was recruited to the position of president of a public company, directly understudying the CEO with the expectation that she would move into that job someday. She was also made a member of the board of directors.

This in itself might not be unusual, but in fact, Doris was the first woman to be given such a job in her area, and it garnered a lot of attention. It was a big deal and she became highly visible. She was even pictured on the cover of one of the trade magazines.

The organizational structure of the company was conventional enough, but there was no chief operating officer. Even though Doris functioned de facto in that role, both she and the chief financial officer reported to the CEO in somewhat parallel positions.

Part of her job as president was to make presentations about the company to analysts and others on Wall Street. This meant having a mastery not only of the operations of the company but of all aspects of "the numbers."

One thing people know about Doris is that she is intellectually curious and she is intellectually competent. Beyond that, when she prepares for a job, she digs in and ensures that she knows as much as she possibly can about the subject at hand.

"I knew that I needed to be thoroughly conversant about everything affecting our operating results and projections," she says, "so I began to look closely at all the numbers."

She was confused by what she found. "I was not basically a financial person, that is, I was not educated specifically in finance or accounting, but I have a good grasp of those disciplines and I'm good with numbers." Still, she was not sure that she was seeing what she thought she saw.

So she asked questions of the CFO. He was evasive. "I remember asking at one point, 'If we're running two million dollars a quarter in general and administrative expenses, why does the projection model say it's going to be five hundred thousand per quarter in quarters three and four?'

"I mean, this was the model we used to base the estimates we gave to the street. I thought he would say, 'Well, it's this or that,' and have some explanation, but he just said, 'Dorrie, it's just an estimate.' "

It seemed something was not right, but Doris kept trying to understand where she herself might be wrong. After all, finance was not her official background.

"I kept trying to add these numbers up and not understanding. I felt that I must be missing something if all the other people at the company weren't seeing what I was seeing. I talked to the auditors and to the company's chief accounting officer."

What Doris discovered, again and again, was that what the CFO told her did not match up with the numbers. "He was lying," she says simply.

Once she found out he was not telling the truth, she started digging deeper and deeper. She discovered that the CFO had intimidated others in the accounting area. "There was an aura of fear and repression in the whole department," she says. "There was a general knowledge that inappropriate things were being done, but when people would ask questions, the CFO would belittle them or make himself seem so smart that they would stop asking questions."

But Doris, as both an attorney and an intellectually competent person, just kept asking the questions and digging. She would not, in her words, "be bamboozled."

Meanwhile, however, Doris's emotional health began to suffer. The stress was just overwhelming. At times she even feared for her physical safety.

She began to question herself. She went through a period of introspection and self-examination. Were there motives she was not admitting? Was she pursuing this because she didn't like the CFO or felt she was somehow competing with him for the top job? Was she on some kind of ego trip?

Basically, this is a healthy response because it is not unusual for people in these situations to try to cook up something to make their rivals look bad. Sad but true.

Consider Doris's position at this point. She was the first woman in this job and she was highly visible; she had to be sure that what she felt she needed to do was completely justified by scrupulous examination of the facts. "Honestly, I thought I was going to have a breakdown. Here I was, I had changed careers and I had thought everything was fine, but now I was sticking my neck out. I had wanted to become a businessperson and knew that if I put my neck on the line in this way, and I was either wrong or overreacting, or if my judgment was wrong about the seriousness of the situation, I would basically have to put my tail between my legs and go back to being a lawyer."

It would have been a failure in a very public and painful way.

One underlying question, of course, was why the CFO was doing these things. Doris could see that he was not personally benefiting in any material way from his behavior. He was not stealing or embezzling. So why indeed was he doing these things?

Doris concluded that it was a simple case of self-aggrandizement, distorting the numbers to make it seem he was achieving the goals the CEO and board had established, even though the achievements turned out to be hollow. Then it probably became a fear of failure.

After preparing herself with the facts, Doris went to the CEO and told him about the actions of the CFO and what she had discovered. At first, he would respond with comments like "Oh he probably forgot that," or "He meant something else." Generally, and probably understandably, he gave the CFO a great benefit of the doubt.

He also reacted that she was being "too technical," or "too concerned about small things." This is a reaction women often face in the workplace—overly concerned with details, the small things, micromanaging, missing the big picture, and so on—and it's a stereotype that tends to stick.

Doris dealt with that directly. She told the CEO, "Look, I know I haven't been with the company my whole life, but I've represented some of the best companies in the business and I know that they will kind of push things around at the margins, but they're not doing this. I know they're not."

And then she said, "There are bad things going on here and we have to tell the board. If we're not going to do that, then I have to resign because I can't associate with this kind of activity."

To the CEO's credit, he agreed to take the matter to the board. The board's reaction? "Hostile and negative. I felt as if they were shooting the messenger."

But the board members quickly realized how dire the situation had become and that Doris was the one they had to depend on to fix it. In a way the CFO's activities, some of which no one but he knew about, had caused the company's financial situation to become almost a house of cards. They were in default on the principal credit agreement and had to tell all this to their lenders. Doris, at the direction of the board, began a process for selling the company.

The stock began to crash. It had been at $47.50 and started downward. Fortunately, two other companies announced that they had bought 5 percent of the company, so, in Doris's words, "we ended up selling for $42 a share, paying off all of our lenders, and maximized the value for all our constituents. It wasn't a big feel-good outcome, but it could have been so much worse."

With that outcome, it could reasonably be expected that the board would be very appreciative. "They never thanked me. I think they just wanted to get away from the whole situation."

Nonetheless, Doris knew she had done the right thing and that it had resulted in the best outcome for the most people. Of course, it could have gone the other way. The CEO could have fired her, or he could have refused to respond, and she would have then been put in the position of making good on her threat to resign. Either way, she could have lost her job.

It's always risky to be the bearer of bad news, and even when you're right, you will likely never feel appreciated for the risk you've taken. It would not even be unusual for you to find yourself blamed for "stirring up trouble" or "making a mountain out of a molehill." Often your only reward is the knowledge that you have been true to your values and you have made the right moral decision regardless of the outcome.

When Doris took the risk, she didn't know whether she'd have to go back to law or get another "business" job. But she maintained her basic optimism, and having come through as bad a situation as she could imagine, she ended up with more confidence in her ability to succeed in the business as well as to be true to her own standards of integrity.

LESSONS TO REMEMBER

- Reject dishonesty regardless of the consequences.
- Be willing to risk your job for the sake of truth.
- Trust your intuition, but do your homework.

FOURTEEN

STICK TO THE VISION OR GO FOR THE MONEY?

The ideals upon which a company is founded can sometimes fall victim to investors who want their money now.

WHEN ASKED, "WHY do you want to go into business?" most entrepreneurs would probably not answer, "To make money while saving the world." When asked, "What's the most important requirement of a new business?" most entrepreneurs would probably answer, "Survival." When asked, "Would you risk going out of business for the sake of preserving your vision, or would you adjust your vision to meet new realities?" most entrepreneurs would probably answer, "Adjust my vision."

Gary Hirshberg is not most entrepreneurs. He is a man who stuck to his very idealistic vision through the most difficult financial and personal circumstances and who passed up financially rewarding opportunities to sell his company until he found the buyer who would maintain the vision. Why? Surprisingly, it is because he believes so deeply in the power of business.

"Listen," he says, "business is the most powerful force on the planet and has the power to either send us where we are headed right now, which I think is to planetary ruin, or to turn it around."

Before coming to this realization, Gary had been running nonprofit organizations trying to save family farms. "But I came to realize that if I wanted to close the gap between people and farmers and help save the planet for my children, I should try to harness the concentrated economic power and opportunity that business provides.

"I wasn't really driven to create a company that was going to save the world all by itself, but I wanted to create a company that was going to show bigger companies how they can make money while saving the world."

So Gary, with the financial support of friends, family, dairy farmers, and others, established Stonyfield Farm, a company specializing in natural and organic yogurt and other dairy products.

Like many new companies, Stonyfield was plagued with a series of calamities. "I didn't know what I was doing for the first nine years," Gary says. "I was struggling to meet payroll every week. I remember one night, after thinking my wife was asleep, tiptoeing over to call my mother-in-law and asking, 'Do you think we could borrow another $5,000 for payroll?' and then hearing the click of call waiting as my wife Meg phoned from the bedroom and said, 'Mom, don't do it.' But she still did it.

"At the end of these years, we ended up being heavily diluted [a term referring to an unusually large number of shares of stock versus the market value of the company] with about three hundred shareholders. It was like an ecosystem in which everything and everybody was connected, and the fact that I knew them all personally meant I could never give up, I could never stop. This was not just about Gary and his mission, but this was a set of human relationships that were very very real. While I had no legal obligation to help them exit and get their money back, I had a moral responsibility to do so."

The question was when. It's reasonable to assume that investors want their money back, plus a good return, as soon as possible after profitability and a period of solid growth.

After the costly learning years, Gary was able to make his vision work, and Stonyfield began to enjoy year after year of good operating results. "I was well into the feeling-my-oats period of enormous growth and effectiveness. By 1997 we'd had our sixth consecutive year of twenty-three-percent annual growth. But the time had arrived for me to come to grips with the desire of my investors for an exit plan. In other words, I had to come up with another financing strategy."

Gary has always considered his company to be, in his words, "an educational institution masquerading as a company." His dilemma was how to provide some kind of buyout plan for the investors while not surrendering his mission to somebody who would not understand or who would abuse it.

"The problem with so many consumer products companies is that they keep making the same mistake of confusing a brand with a values proposition. Brands come and go and depend on continued provocation, intervention, and reinforcement, usually in the form of advertising. Values propositions do not depend on advertising to build a relationship with the consumer or customer. Instead, they create bonds of loyalty and interdependence between the producer and consumer based on mutual appreciation of a common set of values. When consumer products companies go after an acquisition, they typically assume they're buying brands, and as a result those integrations have gone poorly. I just didn't want to be party to that.

"The conventional consumer products company philosophy is to cheapen their products so that they can generate enough gross margin to buy enough gross rating points of advertising to garner market share. The net result is that whoever makes the cheapest stuff then buys the most or the most effective advertising gets the sales. Artificial ingredients like gelatin, modified food starch, fillers, colors, and dyes are cheap shortcuts that avoid the higher costs of real food with real nutrition. But what these brands don't get is customer loyalty. They just get consumption, so they have to play that game over and over again by continuing to buy advertising to support their sales."

Gary explains that his philosophy has been to encode a values proposition into Stonyfield's products. Because he puts real organic and natural food ingredients with real nutritional and ecological value into his cups, Stonyfield's sales come from customer loyalty, not from hit-and-miss advertising. "We get the holy grail of consumer products," he says. "We get product loyalty."

Gary clearly did not want to be bought by the typical large multiproduct consumer goods company, which would try to cheapen his products. He considered taking Stonyfield public, since natural foods companies were getting huge multiples at that time. But after watching a close friend go through that transition, at the end of which the friend realized the company was no longer his and that he no longer controlled its destiny, Gary abandoned that idea.

Meanwhile, Gary was getting pressure for liquidity from some of his investors. "I had one guy in particular who was a real pain in the ass; although I was grateful for his support, he was very exit hungry. He really just wanted liquidity regardless of the consequences to the company. I had to manage all these expectations, but mainly I had to manage my own internal dilemma."

After giving up on going public, Gary engaged an investment banker to find a potential strategic purchaser of his shareholders' stock. "I wanted an entity that would actually respect the mission and the values, one that I could live with and feel was taking my mission to the next level while at the same time living up to my sense of obligation to all the people.

"What I didn't know at the time was that I was starting a two-year process. I learned quickly that I was never going to find an American company to meet my requirements. American companies seem to have the kind of reductionist viewpoint of the world that it all just comes down to numbers.

"Those companies, by the way they talked to me, were just scaring the shit out of me. They kept talking about the opportunity to shrink overhead, which of course is a euphemism for people. And there I was with these incredible employees who had done the impossible. They had enabled this company to survive, then they made it a success. And they were depending on me to do the right thing."

So Gary turned to Europe because he felt that Europeans seem to understand better the connection between commerce, farmers, and the land. But the deal Gary outlined to the investment banker seemed impossible to get from any company, no matter where it was located. The banker said, "This won't happen. No company will go for this."

The conditions?

"I made it clear that I wanted the new owner to buy out all

the nonemployee shareholders, which would be about eighty percent of the company, but I wanted to maintain complete managerial autonomy and control.

"Any employees who wanted to remain shareholders could do so.

"I wanted no veto rights over me.

"I wanted complete independence for as long as I am with the company.

"I was willing to agree to meet certain numbers, but as long as I meet those numbers there would be no interference.

"I wanted autonomy to run this company, but I also wanted entrée to try to bring the influence of our mission to the acquiring company.

"I wanted ten percent of our after-tax profits to continue to go into environmental causes, and I wanted that to continue for no less than a decade after I left the company.

"On top of all that, I wanted the best multiples that had existed to date on any acquisition or integration. I knew them because we had been tracking them closely."

Gary explains that the acquiring company could fire him only for cause, which was defined as not meeting the agreed-to numbers. Of course, there could be other causes, such as malfeasance and so on, but the most likely reason would be a failure to meet the financial goals.

One of the initial meetings with a potential acquirer was with an M&A officer from Groupe Danone, a French multinational dairy company. She was incredulous: "Gary, do you mean to tell me that we may own eighty percent of Stonyfield but that you will still be in control?" Gary said, "Yes."

That conversation was the first in what was to be two years of a raucous and emotional roller coaster ride. At times, Gary recalls, he found himself looking in the mirror and asking, "Am I just bullshitting myself? Am I asking the impossible?"

The two years were spent in meeting after meeting, with some often lasting only a few minutes. "One of the companies I talked with was an American company in our category. Within ten minutes they started talking about the incredible synergies of us combining our facility with their facility.

"First of all, we had the first zero-emissions manufacturing plant in America. By that I mean we were offsetting one hundred percent of our CO_2 from manufacturing. We had a very green process. I had employees who had been involved in profit-sharing and stock options and who had been absolutely underpaid and overworked in the start-up years. And these guys were talking about getting rid of all of them. I just basically said, 'This meeting is over.'"

Gary walked away from the table many times over the two years, during which there was continued contact with Danone in addition to several other companies. Finally, a new representative from Danone, in Gary's words, "saved the deal."

"A guy named Nicholas Moulin had amazing inner strength. He was intent on getting this deal done, and he worked through detail after detail. Our final document was like a phone book when we were done. There were issues like exit multiples, voting control, veto rights, budgets, what constitutes failure, what constitutes cause.

"We invented formulas that stated, for example, if I had two consecutive years of disastrous financial results, that would be cause. But the second year had to be a disaster after the first year. If there was an intervening year with good results, the second bad year would not constitute cause. And so on. It was very complicated.

"I watched Nicholas through all this. He was a master of this stuff, and he knew that time helps to bring parties together. He just would not leave the room but kept saying, 'There is a way to solve this.'

"There were times I wanted to throw in the towel, but cutting to the punch line, I can tell you that now, three years later, everything is working on every single point."

It's a reasonable question to ask why Danone would be so interested in what admittedly was this fairly small American company that they would be willing to negotiate away so much control. That's very unlike most large corporations, which usually expect to consolidate and integrate parts of the two organizations in order to cut costs. Virtually every acquisition has built into the numbers at some point a strategy for combining manufacturing plants or sales forces or distribution centers or even financial and billing operations. So just why was Danone so willing to forgo all those usual acquisition strategies in this case?

Gary says, "I think they knew that with Stonyfield they were getting some intellectual capital they lacked. We knew about the supply chain of organics that they didn't understand. We knew how to talk to the consumer of organic products. And Danone saw the market moving that way, and didn't want their competition to beat them to it. There were a lot of big companies interested in us, and Danone knew that the company that would tolerate this lunatic's desire to keep putting values up front was the company that was going to win this marriage. I think they genuinely valued the know-how we have."

In any process of negotiation there is always strain, always the temptation to compromise more than you intended, always the fatigue factor of ten-hour meetings followed by trying to keep up with the regular responsibilities of managing a company.

But there is a story within this story that moves this situation well beyond the norm. In the middle of the process, Gary's wife was diagnosed with breast cancer and had to begin treatment. In addition, both of his brothers, twins, died of congenital heart defects. Gary was going back and forth from hospital beds and doctors' offices to the negotiating table.

"With the loss of my brothers and with watching the mother of my children going through these exhausting treatments, I had a lot of reasons to pull the ripcord on the parachute and just get out. I was already a rich man. I knew I was going to have plenty of money. So hanging in there on points like keeping our profits for the planet program going or defending my right to decide about new products sometimes seemed less important. There were a lot of reasons to just take the deal and exit."

So why not?

"I hope not to sound high and mighty when I say this, but this is my life's work. I have three children and I'm bringing them into a world that is not pretty. Take any issue, climate change, acid rain, toxins, mercury, et cetera. After working years and years on these issues, I really finally knew that I had found a constructive way to do something useful for my children. I don't mean giving them enough money; I mean that I had found a way to change commerce. That was the reason to stick this out. Otherwise, I'd have to start over and I didn't know if I would have another twenty-five years in me to do this from scratch."

What Gary means is that he has realized in his life the power to change the way business is done. "I realized absolutely that making a strong bottom line and generating cash, throwing off cash at highly competitive multiples was the key to convincing other companies that they could do good and do well at the same time.

"I'm now helping to change the DNA of a multinational company in leading them into this field and into this way of operating."

Is this really true or is Gary just convincing himself and no one else?

"The vindicating moment that told me I had done the right thing by selling to Danone came at the moment we were closing the deal. We had agreed to give the *Wall Street Journal* an exclusive, so I was to go on a conference call with Franck Riboud, the chair and CEO of Danone, and a *Journal* reporter.

"The reporter was going through the usual repertoire of questions you would expect about metrics and numbers, and Franck just cut him off, interrupted him in midsentence. This is verbatim. He said, 'Nick, if you want to judge Stonyfield and this acquisition by the usual financial standards, I assure you you're going to find everything that you want to find because we would never do a deal that was financially not sensible . . . And if you want the conversation to go that way, we'll have our financial people on this phone instead of me.' Then he said, 'But you'd be missing the whole point, because Stonyfield represents an ethic that we at Danone have to adopt if we are going to be successful in the twenty-first century.' "

So how has it worked out?

"We've blown away the numbers. Since the deal closed, we've more than doubled in size."

Gary admits that he'd be a much wealthier man had he kept the company private. "But I've had no regrets," he says. "I've had enormous peace of mind and pride in what we've done."

"In fact," he concludes, "one of the happiest experiences of this entire episode involved a dairy farmer who, years ago, took stock in the company as payment for his milk because we couldn't afford to pay him in cash. He walked away from the deal with a check that was in the six figures. He paid off his farm and paid off his kids' college bills. Nothing could have made me happier."

LESSONS TO REMEMBER

- Persevere on behalf of the things you believe in.
- Resist pressure to go for the easy deal.
- Don't be afraid to change the way business is done.

STAY WITH HIGH QUALITY AND HIGH COST OR CUT THE QUALITY AND LOWER THE COSTS?

When the competition copies your style but not your substance and quality, then underprices you, the decisions get tougher by the day.

MORE AND MORE American businesses these days seem in a race to put quality at the bottom of the value equation. Even companies that built their reputations on quality and value now are too often willing to abandon the commitment to quality, then redefine "value" as simply "low prices."

There is hardly a category of consumer products that has not felt the impact of pricing pressure, and consumers themselves have become conditioned to paying less, or at least to thinking they're paying less. Formerly after-Christmas sales begin before Christmas; seasonal items get "closed out" at the beginning of a season rather than at the end; and there are endless rebating and financing schemes.

When companies find themselves in the squeeze of paying higher costs for raw materials and supplies but unable to raise their prices to the consumer, the first thing that usually gets cut is product quality. Food and beverage companies may change package size, offering less product for the same price, or they may settle for lower-quality ingredients. The airlines are notorious as well for their constant squeezing of seat space and their abandonment of amenities.

And if a company is not willing to meet the demands for lower cost, there always seems to be another company that will. Competition drives the great race downward, and in the face of this bottom feeding, the only possible way to maintain high quality, with commensurately higher prices, is through consumer education. The worry, of course, is that the customers are not paying attention to real qualitative differences these days.

After decades of commitment as the leading producer of high-quality medicinal herb teas, this is the position in which Traditional Medicinals now finds itself: how to educate consumers that quality and efficacy are worth the extra cost.

Fortunately, this is not the first time Drake Sadler, co-founder and CEO, has faced this retaining quality–versus–cost cutting challenge. In fact, you might say he ought to be used to hard choices by now.

In the beginning, Drake and his wife Rosemary (a third-generation herbalist of European background) had a couple of small businesses in northern California. Drake had a graphics design/printing business, and Rosemary had a retail store that sold herbs and herbal products. Though the services and products of their two businesses were very different, their philosophical foundations were the same: They shared the values of social responsibility, environmentalism, and right livelihood.

For example, Drake's printing business featured the use of recycled paper stock, which at the time was much more expensive than virgin paper. And Rosemary sold only the highest-quality herbs and was most interested in educating her customers about the use of medicinal herbs as an alternative to mainstream drugs and medicines. As a dedicated herbalist, her mission was to promote ethical herbalism.

Through her shop, Rosemary also offered various medicinal formulas; for constipation, sore throats, colds and congestion, and so on. Drake also printed herb books and information from Rosemary's classes and lectures. The businesses were small yet sustained their family.

"Rosemary was an herbalist, writer, and educator but was not particularly interested in the business functions," says Drake. "Consequently I did the accounting for the herb store. From the books I could see that there were more and more purchases of herbs, but since it was mostly a cash business, I didn't really have a handle on what was coming in or out of the shop. I remember asking Rosemary questions like, 'Do you need all these herbs?' and 'Do you need a hundred jars of all these varieties?'

"Rosemary's response was often an expression of frustration. She would complain that more people were just coming in to buy her formulas. A dedicated teacher, Rosemary wanted her customers to read herb books and do the formulating work themselves. What her customers wanted, however, were her tasty and effective formulas. So, with some help, Rosemary began to offer these premixed formulas in the jars as well."

In 1973, a family friend came up with the idea to package the formulas into half-pound brown coffee bags in addition to selling them in jars. This packaging idea made it easier for people to get the formulas and assured them that the formulas were consistent in each package. Again, this was somewhat contrary to Rosemary's vision of herbalism, which was to get health-conscious consumers so educated about herbs that they could prepare their own medicines. On the other hand, the information printed on the packaging was an opportunity to educate people on the use of herbs.

Because Drake was in the printing business, he had considerable knowledge of packaging and printed materials. Rosemary assembled the formulas and with some help from a couple of the store clerks made up ten thousand bags of nine tea formulas. The plan was for Drake to travel the West Coast selling the teas in health-food stores for a dollar a bag.

"On my first selling trip, I quickly discovered that Rosemary had such a respected reputation with many of the store owners that we sold all the tea in the San Francisco Bay area within weeks. So the tea business took off, but it wasn't because we had a brilliant business plan or anything like that; people were ready for these medicinal teas, both the health-food retailers and their customers."

How did the business get started and grow with no capital?

"What made the initial start-up phase of the business possible was that Rosemary had good credit with a few herb wholesalers her shop was buying from, and I had good credit with packaging suppliers through my printing business. Consequently, we were able to quickly amass a lot of herbs and packaging even though we didn't have any money. Originally we estimated it would take nine months to sell the first production of ten thousand bags, but instead we sold twenty-five times that amount in the first year. It was incredible."

At this point, the company looked like the great American success story: quality products, environmentally friendly packaging, consumer-friendly product names (such as "Smooth Move" for the laxative tea, "Throat Coat" for the sore throat tea, and so on). But like so many entrepreneurial successes, there are often problems the entrepreneur has never considered. In the case of Traditional Medicinals it was government regulation.

"One day," Drake recalls, "a guy looking like the highway patrol showed up at our small one-room office along the Russian River in Guerneville, which was a real hippied-out area in the northern California forest region. This guy is holding one of our packages of the Smooth Move laxative tea (with an image of an outhouse on the front cover), and he's saying something like, 'You're not fooling anyone with this package. You're making medicines without a license.' And we're thinking, 'Oh God, who's this?' We didn't even know what the Food and Drug Administration was. I had never researched packaging laws or regulatory guidelines or anything like that before."

The FDA agent impressed Drake as serious and threatening, but curiously he visited the company facility only briefly, asked a few questions, took some notes, and then left. Nothing happened for about a year.

"Then we got a very official letter from the California state food and drug authority in which they said very specifically, 'You're making medicines without a license, and the products are in violation of the law.' The letter explained we couldn't use words like 'gentle regularity' or other phrases we used to describe conditions like cold and flu or respiratory ailments. In other words, we couldn't use any of the language that was necessary to describe what the products actually did.

"Understand, we were never in the beverage tea business, we were focused on medicinal herb tea formulas right from the beginning. And there was no question that the products were medicines. Consider this: Forty percent of the world's drugs are made from medicinal plants. For example, three of the largest selling laxatives today are formulated with the herb senna. Senna had always been recognized as an effective laxative, but no company in North America had made a laxative in tea form until we did."

So what would it take to come into compliance with the laws and guidelines? The short answer is an enormous investment and a huge risk. In these early days, Traditional Medicinals' manufacturing facility did not have all the sophisticated drug-compliant laboratory-testing and quality-control equipment. And certainly the funky hip packaging didn't follow the required guidelines for warnings, dosage levels, active ingredients, and so forth. "This had never been done before in North America, and seemed like an insurmountable task to us."

Fortunately, the state regulatory authorities did not mandate a shutdown of the company, so Traditionals' management team had some time, though limited, to respond to the challenge. What began was an exhausting process, including technical research, expensive consultations with regulatory lawyers, face-to-face meetings with the FDA, and long-term strategic planning.

"We had to figure out if what Food and Drug required could even be done, and if so what were the steps and what would be the cost? For instance, the only senna-based laxative products in the market were tablets or syrups. And, just for starters, to be in compliance, we would have to be able to substantiate how much senna was in each dose and how much was safe and effective when you infused it with water as a tea."

At this point in the story, it is important to understand that there was actually a simple solution to this problem. It was the possibility of that simple solution that presented a very difficult dilemma. The solution was to change the commitment and focus of the company and its packaging. Instead of positioning these products as medicinals, reposition them as foods. Instead of making specific claims about product efficacy, make general claims. Instead of labeling a product like Smooth Move as an effective stimulant laxative, just say it is for overnight relief. Instead of saying the cold medicine is a decongestant, say that it's helpful to drink during the cold season. There are several wellness-type tea companies in the market today that have successfully gone down this path of least resistance.

And the name of the company? Simple. Change it from Traditional Medicinals to Traditional Herbals. No laboratory needed, no investment in research and testing, no changes on the packaging. *Voilà!* Problem solved.

But Drake knew that this simple solution was just not consistent with the company's mission and its commitment to promoting and educating about the benefits of traditional herbal medicine.

"It was an ethical dilemma and it put our integrity to the test. We could have easily positioned the products as foods and marketed them without the claims. I also knew that the decision to go forward and to continue marketing products as medicines would put the company at risk. This approach had never been done before, and there was no guarantee that it could be done. It was a huge gamble, and if our strategy was unsuccessful, we would be left with a shell of a company, with no resources (since the regulatory research and facility investment would be very expensive) and with dumbed down products that we wouldn't feel comfortable producing.

"The problem was ethical: If we couldn't label our products with their health benefits, we would be sacrificing our integrity, which was the company's reason for being. From the very beginning our mission was to educate consumers about the medicinal benefits of herbs with the packaging."

So Traditional Medicinals carved out the difficult path, made the necessary regulatory, packaging, and infrastructure and facility investments, was ultimately licensed by the state, and became the first and only herb company in North America to market its products as natural medicines. This elevated the company's status in the natural products industry and opened up new channels of distribution into supermarkets and drugstores. The overall result of the decision to stick with the company's vision was positive, but the cost of this investment is still being felt decades later.

"We spent, and still spend, all of our money on lawyers, clinical trials, laboratory testing, quality control, the most expensive medicinal-grade herbs, packaging, and so on. In the process we didn't spend that money on marketing or new products and revenue generating activities that would have propelled the business farther at a lower cost. And the path we took has resulted in much higher costs to this day."

Which brings this story up to date and to the dilemma now facing Traditional Medicinals. As the company, its products, and the medicinal tea category have become established, numerous competitors have aggressively entered the market. Of course, this is no surprise and is to be expected in any growth category of products. But here's the difference: The competitors have adopted similar positioning but not a similar investment in quality.

"They market their teas as foods and not medicine, they

avoid the built-in costs that Traditional Medicinals incurs with its sophisticated manufacturing facility, and they use low-quality herbal ingredients.

"With the now more relaxed regulatory environment, these brands can make wellness-type claims for their products, and they adopt product names much like ours. However, when a knowledgeable herbalist looks at their formulations, there's no rhyme or reason for their products other than the fact that they are flavored in order to be pleasant-tasting beverages that mask the low-quality herbs they use. This allows them to market for flavor, lifestyle, and price but not efficacy! They just imply efficacy with crafty marketing.

"This creates a difficult competitive marketplace for us because it's not an even playing field, and it's easy for these low-quality competitors to gain market share because they can afford to promote on price. And after all, the average consumer often doesn't take time to read the labels, and when he or she sees two products that seem to offer the same benefits, the choice will always be the one that's cheaper."

The question now is how will the company continue to compete against other brands that don't demonstrate the same level of ethical concern? How will the company differentiate itself from its competitors?

There are few answers at this point, but Drake is optimistic. "One of the real benefits of having seized the high road and never wavering is that we have this tremendous wealth of commitment within the company. The people here are so dedicated to Traditional Medicinals because they believe in what we do. And I think that's rare in companies. Other than the products, our greatest assets are the people who work at Traditional Medicinals along with the many dedicated people we work with outside of the company. The veterans of the natural products industry are proud to partner with us.

"Occasionally someone new in the company will ask, 'Why do we buy only the most expensive pharmaceutical herbs when their high costs raise our prices in the marketplace?' What's most rewarding to me is the understanding and ethical response that comes uniformly from the other employees to these kinds of challenging questions."

But Drake has no illusions about what's ahead. "I can't say I know exactly what to do about low-price competitors other than not to waver from the company's quality commitment and vision, on the belief that in the end we will have achieved something great, a sustainable organization with lasting value and values.

"The question is whether the consumers will understand and appreciate the value proposition sooner rather than later and be willing to pay for real medicine as opposed to flavored wellness tea. That's the one I really struggle with. I'm impatient with change, and I would like to more fully witness the renaissance of ethical herbalists in my lifetime."

What is very clear is that Drake is not tempted to violate his sense of integrity and join the great race to the bottom. Thus, this story continues even as you read these words.

LESSONS TO REMEMBER

- Have confidence that keeping your commitments to high standards will build enormous employee loyalty and support.
- Be aware that the marketplace is not always a level playing field.
- Research all the government rules and regulations before you plunge into a new venture.

SIXTEEN

PROTECT YOUR CAREER
OR DO YOUR DUTY?

It's amazing how your career can take a big hit from
standing up to a senior officer's threat.

MILITARY AND CIVILIAN organizations are far more similar than dissimilar. An air force wing and army battalion are like corporations, made up of smaller operating units, each with its job to do in order to support the overall goals of the greater organization. They are managed and led, most often, in a hierarchical setting with various levels of authority indicated by titles: "Department Head" or "Vice President" in a corporation; "Captain," "Major," "Colonel," or "Commander" in the military.

Each publishes policies and procedures, each emphasizes standards of quality and productivity, each has reward systems based on objective appraisal and critique of individual performance, and each has its politics.

There's one big difference: Corporations are not dealing in the daily possibility of death and destruction, whereas in the military its "employees" strive constantly to perfect their ability to do what they hope they will never have to do.

For many pilots in the air force during the threatening years of the cold war, that meant being ready to navigate precisely over great distances and, if called upon by presidential order, to drop their nuclear weapons in exactly the right place at exactly the right time.

Making sure that pilots' skills were honed to this level of perfection is one of the jobs of an air force flight examiner, a fellow pilot who flies in a chase plane and evaluates another pilot's performance. It was in this role that Tom Sawner had to choose between his duty and his personal advancement.

Despite this incident, it should be noted that Tom did very well in the air force, and several years later was given the Anthony Shine Award as the most outstanding fighter pilot in the air force. This is a designation reflecting not only flying skill but also intelligence, decision-making, and judgment.

For anyone who knew Tom, this achievement was not a surprise. His father had been a fighter pilot, and all Tom ever wanted to do was fly fighters. He didn't even bother to apply to any colleges beyond the Air Force Academy. "Given how selective they are," he admits now, "that was probably a dumb thing to do."

But he was selected, graduated, and went into pilot training. At the time only the top 10 percent were selected for fighters. Tom was among those. He continued to excel and, as a young captain, advanced in his skills well ahead of his peers. This resulted in his being named one of his wing's flight examiners. This is where the story really begins.

At the time, the cold war was raging, with various wings of the air force standing by on alert to possibly drop nuclear weapons. This was probably the highest-pressure job at the time; thus it was critical that the pilots who were to be ready to go to war at a moment's notice be the most qualified pilots in the air force. Part of Tom's job as flight examiner was to give check rides to ensure that the nuclear-qualified pilots were at the highest level of readiness.

"Getting those check rides done was a really big deal for all the pilots," he says. "It was part of a very extensive certification to make sure that you were qualified, competent, and had integrity.

"The standards were very very tight because if, God forbid, this should ever happen, that there was a nuclear exchange with the Soviet Union, there would be nuclear weapons coming from ICBMs, from submarine-launched missiles, as well as from fighter pilots like me flying fighters. So it was very important that the pilot be exactly where you're supposed to be exactly on your time schedule."

So what were the standards for a check ride?

Tom explains that there were basically three levels of qualification, with level two meaning the pilot had some discrepancies but not enough to fail and level three being a failure. "A Qual level three meant that you had to go through remedial training. It was felt to be a huge black mark on your record because you were decertified as someone qualified to stand alert."

The pilots Tom was checking were flying F-4 Phantoms at low levels, about five hundred feet above the ground, for several hundred miles at eight nautical miles a minute. Navigation was strictly the old-fashioned kind, without radio aids. After all, during a war, there would be no handy radio aids to help you find the target, and this was well prior to deployment of the satellite Global Positioning System, which provides such precise navigation today.

In addition, the routes were ones not usually flown. "We saved certain routes for check rides so that people wouldn't become too familiar with them because in the real world, this would be a first look. After all, you don't get to practice flying to the actual target."

Standards were very tight: To earn Qual level one, the pilot would be required to arrive at each turn point within fifteen seconds of the appointed time. Thirty seconds or more meant an automatic Qual level two. Two minutes, a very long time at five hundred miles per hour, was an automatic bust.

Also, the pilot's path over the ground could not deviate over one half mile either side of the center line of his course. Tom explains that the flight examiners were allowed a certain amount of judgment. If a pilot deviated outside the half mile but quickly corrected and got back on course, that might be considered acceptable. If he did that several times, it might add up to a major discrepancy. "But there were hard-and-fast rules we were not allowed any judgment in. If the pilot got two miles or more from his route for any amount of time, it was an automatic Qual level three. No questions, no exceptions."

Tom explains that it was fairly rare for a pilot to flunk a check ride. "Most of these pilots were very professional and prided themselves on their skill and training. I remember missing a turn point by five seconds once and I was appalled at myself."

It was with a certain amount of concern that Tom learned he was to give a check ride to a senior officer who had recently come from a tour as a staff officer (which means he had not been serving specifically as a combat-ready pilot). "The rumor mill before he got there was that he had a high sponsorship with multiple generals and was on track for promotion as a general. But people who have those kinds of political aspirations in the military still have to go back into the field from time to time. It is said that you build your mentors on the staff and not out in the field, so many of them spent their time where they figured it would do their careers the most good, which was on the staff. Most of us flying fighters out in the field didn't have a lot of respect for the 'staff weenies,' which is ironic because two assignments later, I was one myself. But that's another story."

Tom says that the senior officer's skills were pretty rusty, but because he was destined to be a commander, he needed to get his skills up to date.

"The check ride mission is planned as if it is a real mission. The pilot has to answer questions that the flight examiner poses about potential threats along the way, such as surface-to-air missiles, what kind of evasive action to take, and so on. This is done with an oral exam and it went okay, so we saddled up and took off."

The early part of the mission went well enough, within time and distance on the first couple of turn points. "But then he got to a turn point in the middle of the route and just flew right past it. He also flew past the time he should have turned. The rule is if you don't see the checkpoint but reach your turn time, turn anyway."

The senior officer went several miles past the checkpoint, then finally turned. "Unfortunately, now he was flying parallel to his course and more than two miles off where he should be. He was convinced that he was on course, but he flew past the next checkpoint a little bit, and when he didn't see what he expected to see, turned anyway. All this compounded itself on the next two checkpoints. He finally figured out where he was, looped around, and found the target, but he was two minutes and forty-something seconds late. At this point, my hands as flight examiner were absolutely tied."

For Tom, the evaluation was not a difficult call. It was clear that he had busted the check ride. "I figured he knew absolutely he'd blown it because he had to know how much time he was off. And this was independent of the fact that he'd overflown a turn point enough to be considered a bust.

"Understand, this was not a career-killing kind of thing. It meant he'd have to take several different training flights to get back into practice and was decertified until then."

Before the debriefing, Tom had called his superior officer as he always did. "Plus, I wanted to give him a heads-up. You know, this was a senior officer and a commander. So I said to my boss, 'I think this is pretty cut and dried. I'll have to give him a Qual level three.' The response was not extraordinary. My boss said he was sorry it happened, but he completely concurred. We all knew these things happen from time to time."

But what Tom learned was that this upwardly mobile senior officer did not want to have even the slightest black mark on his record. "Usually at a mission debriefing it's understood that we check, or in other words, leave our rank at the door. We're not talking about anything that has to do with rank; we're talking about the ability to do the assigned mission within the required standard, and it really doesn't matter whether you're the youngest lieutenant or the most senior general. This is serious stuff because we're simulating nuclear weapons and there's nothing more serious than that. That's why the criteria were so cut and dried."

But the senior officer did not leave his rank at the door. He denied that he'd made the errors and said that the airplane had malfunctioned. Tom persisted and finally the senior officer said, "We need to talk privately." With just the two of them present, he continued, "I can't afford to have a bust. I'm going to be a general and I don't want this on my record, plus it will make me look bad in the squadron."

Tom responded, "Sir, I'm terribly sorry, but this isn't a judgment call. If it was a judgment call, I'd do everything I could to work things out, but my hands are tied."

"You can call it a 'no check,' " the officer said.

"But I can't because there's no criteria or reason for that," Tom said.

Then came the blow. "If you let this stand, Captain, you won't go anywhere in this wing. You need to go talk to your boss before you write this up." At this point, Tom could have decided to reclassify the check flight as a "no check," bending the rules a bit but not breaking any regulations. "But it would not meet the standards that I had sworn to uphold, or have been fair to all the other pilots for whom we did not bend the rules," says Tom. "I just couldn't live with that."

So Tom agreed to call his boss, knowing that his boss would agree with him that the flight was a bust. As Tom recalls, "My boss was a great guy and a top fighter pilot. I really respected him. He was upset at the inappropriate pressure and told me to 'be careful, this guy has a reputation.' "

Then Tom's boss, acting as many good leaders would, offered to take the heat himself. He said, "Why don't you tell him it was my call and that I decided it was a bust?"

Tom appreciated the offer but replied, "Thanks, sir, but it was my ride and it's my call, I just wanted to give you a heads-up and to make sure you agreed with my call."

Tom returned to the senior officer and said, "I'm sorry, sir, but this is the way it's going to stand."

"It's your career," was the response.

A few months later, as luck and Murphy's Law would have it, Tom was assigned to fly as a flight examiner with the squadron this same officer was commanding. He called Tom into his office.

"Well, Tom," he said, "what goes around comes around."

"He was not in a position to do anything to me," says Tom, "but at one point he did suggest that I was a poor officer and that I'd be better off resigning from the air force. I took that advice with a grain of salt."

As luck would have it, the commander got his retribution. Tom had excelled in every way in his career up to that point and was in line for an early promotion to major. By happenstance, this same senior officer was in a wing staff position at the time Tom's promotion recommendation was making its way through the system. Despite an absolutely superb rating by Tom's direct superior, this same senior officer killed Tom's early promotion by writing a very negative endorsement to his performance evaluation.

"I thought there had been a big mistake because we had a new wing commander, so I went to talk to the new commander and he sent me back to this same guy, and he said, 'I told you before, Tom, "What goes around comes around." ' And that was that."

Tom admits that while he knew there was some risk to his career involved, he couldn't have suspected at the time of the check ride that this man would have gone so far as to torpedo his early promotion. "But it wouldn't have mattered," he says, "because the deal is the deal. There can't be tolerance of incompetence in those circumstances regardless of rank or career or anything else."

And finally, Tom's confidence in the air force was affirmed when he heard that this commander, the man who tried to bully him and who killed his early promotion, never made it to general after all. During a follow-up assignment at the

Pentagon, he was fired from a significant position, moved to another one lower down in the organization, and given a very negative performance appraisal.

Tom's comment: "I guess what goes around actually does come around."

LESSONS TO REMEMBER

- Don't be intimidated by authority.
- Don't be argued out of doing what you know to be the right thing.
- Don't tolerate incompetence under any circumstances.

SEVENTEEN

DO THE HARD RIGHT OR SETTLE
FOR THE EASY WRONG?

*It's easy enough to "let the buyer beware," but the
problem is living with yourself.*

THE GREAT DUALISM in the world of work in America is that
we have often let ourselves become two different people, one
person at work and another at home, meaning that we hold
to one set of values at home and another at work.

We also are capable of separating our personal values from
the values of our organizations, as if what we do in the name
of business is entirely different from what we do in our own
names. The refrain "It's just business" becomes the justification for any number of things we wouldn't accept in our personal lives. In some circles it is even considered naive to
believe that a business must operate as an extension of the
values of its people. And it seems that the higher we go in organizations, the easier it is to rationalize behaviors that we
once would have considered misleading if not outright dishonest.

But to be fair, these situations are not always easy judg-
ments to make. If the behaviors are not clearly illegal, they

fall under the less easily defined category of organizational ethics, which means that they finally get down to how the people of an organization have agreed to behave. Thus, the "rules" become an internal discipline guided by colleagues and peers.

This moral agreement among colleagues underpins the kind of organization that Chip Baird created with North Castle Partners, a private equity firm. North Castle buys companies and works with the management to create value and build the business. After some period of time, typically three to five years, the companies are sold again at a profit which is returned to the investors in North Castle.

Chip is the CEO. He not only tries to live his values personally but insists that North Castle Partners also live its values. The creed of the firm is "Value & Values."

The conventional wisdom holds that the number one value for a private equity company, as it would be for, say, a venture capitalist, is return on investment. Financial return on investment trumps everything else.

Chip affirms that North Castle is certainly committed to a good return on investment for its partners and investors, but—and this is what makes all the difference for Chip—not at the sacrifice of its integrity. The "how" is as important as the "how much."

It would be one thing to take this position as a stable company with years in the business and many deals in its history, but in this story Chip was leading North Castle in one of its earliest deals. The choices he faced could literally have meant the success or failure of the firm.

"This was one we worked on really before we had money in the bank," he says. "If we could make this deal work, it would launch us to the next level of our business."

Chip had his eye on a company called Vital Life Functional Foods (a fictional name), which sold "healthy beverages" to the specialty market. When Chip became interested, the company was doing about $150 million in business a year.

Chip met with the company's owner and together they developed a vision. "We wanted to take this business," Chip says, "as we put it, from the island to the mainland, the mainland being the mass market and the island being the specialty market.

"This strategy would require a lot of investment, including building a new brand, bringing in thirty new members of management, and spending about ten million dollars in new systems so we could be a supplier to Wal-Mart." A deal was agreed to and North Castle bought Vital Life Foods.

The core of the business was "healthy beverages," which translates into drinks sold as meal supplements for active people.

"They're filled with protein," explains Chip, "so in a world where protein becomes critically important, you can have a high-protein, low-carb drink and feel full without having to eat a tuna sandwich with mayonnaise."

The new management team successfully completed the transformation and did an extraordinary job of building the business.

"It had gone so well that, after about five years of ownership, North Castle was within a few months of selling the company and getting liquidity for its investors. At this point that had become very important, because North Castle had not given any money back to its investors. It needed to have a successful transaction and return some money to its investors.

"In the private equity business, your customers ultimately

want their money back, more like two or three or four times their money back."

There was unusually intense pressure at this time, about 2003 and 2004, because investors were still suffering from the downturn after the crash of 2000.

"Some of our investors had lost extraordinary amounts of money in other investments, so liquidity was important to them. The whole tenor of the industry had changed, so that what became most vital for our customers, our investors, was liquidity. And of course it was critically important for North Castle, so much so that we couldn't even think about raising another fund until we sold Vital Life. So all our resources were focused on making that happen."

Considering the success of the new brands and the general growth of Vital Life, selling the company should have been a slam dunk. A sale and a great return for everyone seemed a foregone conclusion.

But something happened that was to challenge the very foundation of the values and the integrity of North Castle.

Chip starts the story this way: "One of our partners who was close to the team at Vital Life began to hear that one of the top executives was playing very fast and loose with using corporate resources for personal purposes. Understand that this was an incredibly successful executive. But he'd done a whole range of things, from renting ski chalets for his personal use to chartering airplanes for his family, and so on."

But aren't these things that companies often do to entertain big customers?

"Of course," says Chip, "and he would say it was for customers or for a prize for a top salesperson, but it turned out that wasn't the case. He'd rent a one-hundred-foot yacht that would entertain customers for one night and then use it personally for the next three days. There was a whole range of those kinds of things."

The point can be made, and has been made by many top executives, that anything that saves them time or provides respite from the pressures of their jobs qualifies as a legitimate business expense.

"Some people might say it's gray," Chip says, "and that executives do it all the time, that everybody does it."

Isn't it true that trying to judge what are simple perquisites for senior people and what is corruption is pretty complicated?

For Chip, it was "absolutely black-and-white. We often talk in our partnership group about these kinds of values, and we talked about this situation."

After a long discussion with his partners, Chip took some time away to think about what to do. He asked one of his partners to do an investigation and put together all the facts. "You could say that any one of these incidents alone would not have been so bad, but the sum total of them was egregious enough that I concluded we had to do something."

Chip told his partnership group that to let the executive's behavior stand without the most severe penalty, which included termination and the loss of millions of dollars of stock options, would "make our company values a travesty."

Strong words. Chip got some pushback and serious questions from some partners, and for seemingly good reason. The executive was a star, he had made the company successful. In addition, the sale of the company was looming and if the executive was fired, that would mean delaying the sale and perhaps even severely undermining its value to a potential buyer, thus lowering the return on investment for all.

Of course, Chip could have proceeded with the sale and let

the new buyer worry about the executive and his problems. Many executives, under these kinds of pressures, would have done just that and would have, as the phrase goes, "let the buyer beware."

"But for me," Chip says, "this is one of those decisions a chief executive makes. You can listen to people's advice, and I did, but there was never a question in my mind what the right thing to do was. I knew I had to opt for the hard right rather than just take the route of the easy wrong."

This situation put a sudden and unexpected pressure on everyone but most particularly on Chip, who felt as if it was all riding on his shoulders and that the company's very existence was in the balance.

"In making this decision there was no question that we were putting our firm at risk, because we had no other company in the portfolio that was ready to sell. All of our shareholders expected us to sell Vital Life; we'd told them as much, so the expectations were incredibly high. If I followed through with this decision, it meant not selling Vital Life, at least until this whole management situation was sorted out. If we'd had someone ready to step into this executive position, the situation would not have been so critical, but we didn't have anyone ready. In my mind the delay could have been six months to a year, which certainly would have lowered the value of the deal and literally threatened our survival.

"But to me, value and values go together. We call it the genius of the ampersand. It's like cost and quality. You can have both. It's not a trade-off. Value and values together."

How did the partners feel about it? After all, it's their risk as well.

"I would say that to some of the partners it was a much

more ambiguous decision. One of them said, 'You're crazy. Don't you know you're putting everything at risk?' But I felt that if we couldn't live by our values, then we were no different from a thousand other private equity firms."

The next step in the process was to call in the executive and confront him with the results of the investigation.

"The meeting lasted at least an hour and a half," recalls Chip, "because I believe you have to go through the data carefully. For this man, crossing the line ethically meant the potential loss of millions of dollars even though he would have a generous severance package. But not to take him through all the facts would not have been fair.

"So I started the meeting by telling him we had a very serious problem. We had sorted the issues into three areas: absolutely black-and-white fire-able offenses, gray areas that could be debated either way, and minor offenses. We concentrated on the first group.

"I told him that we wanted to take him through these things, then let him talk about them and help us understand what had happened. I did not just come out and say you're terminated because I really hoped that he would have an explanation for some of these things."

The executive's initial response was denial, or he would say things like, "I was going to bring the painting back from my living room to the company." Then his attitude turned to incredulity: "Look, I'm the most successful executive in the North Castle portfolio. How can you possibly bring me down over a jet ride or a boat or some paintings?"

As recent revelations about high-profile CEOs have demonstrated, it seems a psychology of entitlement often develops in those admittedly high-pressure jobs. But Chip was having none of it.

"About halfway through the meeting, after a lot of squirming and his third or fourth attempt to create some story that then was refuted by the facts, the executive became very sullen because he knew he'd been caught."

After the meeting, Chip chose to help protect the man's dignity, thus did not make an announcement that spelled out the details of his leaving. "That would not have been the appropriate way to get the message out," he says.

In any company at any point, but particularly in this company at this time, Chip's choice was probably the most difficult a leader can face. What was the reaction from the rest of the company?

"I would say that the North Castle family understood very quickly what had happened and why. And actually, I think most of our partners felt incredibly proud. It was also a very powerful statement to the associates in the firm that the values on the wall actually mean something."

What about financial impact?

"We think a lot of things through using the foil of value and values.

"On the values side, this was one of the most powerful examples that our values mean something. When you're willing to put the firm at risk over your concept of what integrity is in the behavior of a executive, it's a strong signal.

"On the value side, this action was a looming disaster because we had to scramble. We had to think of how long it was going to take to figure out whether the next guy in line could take over and whether that meant we couldn't sell the business for a year or was it six months, and so on. On the value side, it created enormous anxiety within the company."

Chip promoted a man who had been living in the former executive's shadow for a long time and, as it turned out, had learned a lot about the business. Thus, the sale came only six months later than the original timing.

How about price?

"I think it ultimately affected the price," says Chip, "but only indirectly because of the termination. The later timing put the company up against the enormous boom of the low-carb phenomenon. It was just overwhelming the nutrition market, so Vital Life, while it had a product line that fit, was really trying to grow into a pretty stiff wind. The longer that went on, the weaker Vital Life's results became."

Chip is candid in admitting that the business sold for perhaps as much as $50 million less than it would have earlier. "But we still got a reasonable return," he says. "We still got two and a half times our money, so in general it was a pretty good investment over five years. It could have been better, but not at the cost of sacrificing our integrity."

And he adds, "For the company and its commitment to values as well as value, I'd call it a happy ending all the way around."

LESSONS TO REMEMBER

- Recognize that sticking to your values in the face of adverse circumstances can inspire everyone in your organization.
- Be willing to take the long-term difficult choices instead of taking the path of least resistance.
- Never tolerate unethical behavior in any employee regardless of title, position, or accomplishments.

EIGHTEEN

SUPPORT A COLLEAGUE OR THINK ONLY OF YOURSELF?

Sometimes a routine workaday situation can put you in an ethical tight spot.

WE TEND TO think that the greatest work challenges to our integrity will involve such weighty matters as the relative morality of laying off people versus risking great financial loss, or confronting issues of financial manipulation versus just hoping the auditors or tax people won't discover the problems—all those things we read about in the newspapers.

But it is far more likely that sometime during the most routine day at work, you will find yourself caught by surprise in an ordinary, everyday situation that puts your integrity to the test. In fact, for most of us, it is these daily choices and decisions that define our sense of ethics and how we manifest our integrity at work.

It was during one of those ordinary days while in a routine meeting that Amanda Kuhr (not her real name) found herself at a moment of truth. Her problem began the day before in another routine meeting when a colleague asked her to listen to, and critique, a presentation he was to make the next day to the management group.

This is one of those favors people do for one another, so naturally Amanda agreed. She was positively impressed and, with the exception of a few minor suggestions, gave her colleague very encouraging feedback.

During the meeting the next day, Amanda noted to her satisfaction that her colleague had incorporated her minor suggestions into his presentation. She thought it went well; then came the shock.

Members of the management group began to sharply criticize the presentation. "It was unanimous and it was beyond mere criticism," Amanda recalls. "It was almost brutal. They picked it apart point by point, including the minor suggestions I had made."

As her colleague tried to defend his work, he looked to her for support, and suddenly what had been the most routine of situations became a critical challenge for Amanda. She had liked the presentation, but everyone else hated it. If she spoke up and supported her colleague, she would become identified with what the others considered substandard work; thus she would risk her own reputation with the group. If she did not support her colleague, she would do great damage to their relationship, and more important, it would be a personal ethical failure.

It's easy to shrug off situations like this as insignificant or unimportant. "So what's the big deal?" some will ask. She doesn't have to say anything; she can just keep quiet, right? Her colleague will understand the position she's in.

But what if her colleague tells the group that Amanda saw the presentation and liked it? If Amanda were willing to stretch things a bit she could say, "When I saw it yesterday it was in a slightly different form, and I liked it, but I see today that it just doesn't work." That might be a little misleading, but it wouldn't be dishonest. She did see it in a slightly different form, right? And she could try to explain herself to the colleague later.

Many people would find either of these "solutions" acceptable in the scheme of things, but that's because they are willing to redefine these situations as matters of workaday expediency rather than as ethical issues.

Amanda did not keep quiet, nor did she dissemble. She said, "I admit I'm surprised by everyone's response. I saw this presentation yesterday and I thought it was very effective, but I have so much respect for the opinions of this group that I have to reexamine my own opinion." She then pointed out some of the positive things she still felt about the presentation and offered to work with her colleague to make it acceptable to the others.

In having the courage to be honest against the pressure of the group, she preserved her relationship with the colleague and, she adds, "I think the others ended up respecting me for going against the tide as I did."

LESSONS TO REMEMBER

- Realize that even the most routine situations can become a challenge to your integrity.
- Have the courage to express your opinion even when it differs from everyone else's.

NINETEEN

GO ALONG AND GET ALONG OR RESCUE THE COMPANY CULTURE?

Succession planning in family business is difficult to begin with and is made even worse when there's a culture clash.

FAMILY-OWNED COMPANIES have problems all their own. True, they are free from the pressures of Wall Street and the threats of hostile takeover and the prospect of angry stockholder meetings, but in the critical area of succession planning, their problems are unique.

They normally do not have a succession planning process in place, as most publicly held corporations do. Management consultants who focus their practice on family-owned companies identify three basic succession situations in which problems can arise: (1) The founder/entrepreneur is so successful that the company outgrows his or her management ability, but there is a reluctance to bring in professional management to preserve the company's success; (2) the founder/entrepreneur is ready to withdraw and, understandably, passes along the management responsibilities to a younger member of the family who may not be qualified to handle them; (3) the founder/

entrepreneur tries a combination of family and professional management, thus creating control issues that can easily result in conflict.

In the first case, the founder just doesn't realize his or her deficiencies, often until the company begins to suffer. In the second, family pride trumps professional judgment to the detriment of the company. In the third, it is essential that both family member and professional manager be qualified and compatible.

It was the third situation in which Leslie Lundgren (not her real name) found herself a few years ago. She had a law degree, she had a job, and she was happy in Chicago. She did not have a fixed plan for the rest of her life, but she never imagined that she would have to return to her hometown, enter the family business, encounter and face down a nasty management situation, then become CEO and reinvigorate the company's culture.

The catalyst was her father's illness, which had caused him to slowly become less active and to turn the company's management over to a trusted adviser and colleague.

Sometime after that, on a family vacation, Leslie's father told her he'd like her to become part of the company management. "It was a surprise, to say the least," Leslie says. "He didn't come right out and say it, but as we talked I could tell that my father had developed serious doubts about his top management guy and that the illness kept him from being as involved as he would have liked."

Her father had always managed the company very personally and he had never developed a succession plan, plus there were not the usual systems of accountability, thus creating a situation that was ripe for abuse. "In effect," Leslie says, "we're talking about a situation in which the top person could do basically whatever he wanted with whatever money he wanted.

"Dad didn't feel that he was able to stay up-to-date, and he worried that management didn't have anyone involved from the ownership side anymore. In other words, he wanted someone from the family back into the management of the business."

Leslie's father could have brought Leslie into the picture earlier, of course, but he knew the pitfalls of family companies, which can easily become so ingrown that nothing new or innovative is ever introduced. Far too many family companies lose their vitality because they tend to do what has always "worked," then become simply an employment resource for all the family offspring.

Leslie's father had brought in a professional manager because he wanted to avoid that trap. He knew that in order to grow, to respond to shortened business cycles and the demands of the market, his company had to remain innovative in both product development and improvement as well as in marketing.

But after four years, it wasn't working as he had hoped, so he chose to reach out to Leslie. She was generally informed about the business and had spent her growing-up years in and around the company and its people, but she was uncomfortable with what her father wanted her to do. The first thing she asked was, "How will John [the president, not his real name] feel about my doing this? I have a law degree, not an MBA, so what qualifications do I have?"

But her father convinced Leslie that she should come into the company as a representative of the family, calling her "Asset Manager for the Family." Her father explained to John that "I want Leslie to learn more about day-to-day operations and be able to provide some link back to the ownership as well as help implement my estate plan."

In this role, Leslie understood that she was charged with the responsibility of "making sure that things were in place . . . the usual stuff, reducing taxes, making sure my mother would be okay, and so on."

What made this situation more complicated than a normal family member/professional manager arrangement, however, was Leslie's uncertainty about whether her father suspected that his president, who was also his accountant, was acting with the best interests of the company in mind.

If she was expected to determine that and do something about it, she felt there had to be a clear understanding from the beginning about authority and control issues. "I wanted to be nonthreatening," she says, "but at the same time I told my Dad that I would need to have some legitimate authority. Otherwise I would just be the kid whose Dad gave her a job. I felt strongly that I needed to be able to assist in strategic planning for the company. I mean, after all, how could I be asset manager for the family and not have some say in how the family's major asset was being managed?"

Good question. But what does this mean for the existing management team and what should their response be? In this case, the top guy had been charged with creating a process that would lead to selling the company, and part of his compensation package included a particular bonus for that activity.

So Leslie's hope was that John would see an advantage to the company and to himself by considering her a partner in getting the company ready for the next phase of its life and development.

It was not to be. The more she learned, the greater the problem became. One of the first things the president told her was that he did not want her salary coming out of his bottom line.

"Control freak doesn't even begin to describe him," says Leslie. "I quickly discovered that the employees who had been so carefully and sensitively nurtured by my dad were now being managed by fear. Yet this man had been chosen by Dad, he was president, and he had been doing a reasonable job of running the company. And I was not only the newcomer but also the boss's kid."

Her concerns were exacerbated by her need for information and analysis. "The president made it clear that he resented my presence and felt he did not owe me any information. This was within forty-eight hours of my arriving on the scene. So I needed to sit back, try to regroup, and determine the right thing to do. Crying and whining about a problem is not my style, so I needed to figure out a way to get information because he had made that incredibly difficult."

So often in these situations it is the professional manager, the "outsider," who faces defensiveness on the part of family members and who has difficulty getting the information needed for good management. In this case, it was the family member who was treated as the intruder.

It turned out that Leslie had one big advantage: the legacy of her father. He was an intuitive manager who kept his door open to all employees and who encouraged a lot of cross-functionality. Leslie realized that the employees saw her presence as a recommitment on the part of the family and that they were eager to communicate with her.

"It goes back to my childhood," she says. "Some of the older employees remember me hanging around the plant when I was a little girl." Leslie saw these connections as an avenue for learning the business and gathering information.

She preferred to learn the state of the business by working with the president and was uncomfortable with the thought that, by seeking other sources, she would be circumventing him. She also did not want to be seen as trying to split employee loyalties.

"So I decided the first thing I needed to do was simply solidify relationships with people. I certainly had very little knowledge about the workings, the ins and outs of manufacturing and the processes and procedures for how things got done from beginning to end."

She began, department by department, to learn. She spent time with everybody, asking questions: "What do you do? What do you see? What do you think we should do better?"

The first shift began at 6 A.M.; Leslie was there. "For me it was just practical. I had to figure out what the heck was going on. I didn't have an MBA, I didn't come with thirty years of experience in some other industry, but I do have a passion for figuring out how things work. And, like my father, I like people and I believe I have a gift of making people feel comfortable."

As positive as these activities were and as positive an effect as they had on the employees, they were bound to be seen by the president as threatening to his authority. His style could not have been more different. Leslie describes him as a "quiet dictator" who didn't really want people communicating and who generally ignored his employees.

"He never walked around the plant, never said hello, didn't seem to like people. I bet you could count on one hand the number of times he walked through the whole office and said 'Hi.' "

Leslie also discovered that he had fired most of the people

who had been close to her father, a not-too-unusual power play: Throw out the old team, bring in your own.

This treatment of employees struck Leslie as not only unfair and unethical but also dumb management. "Listen," she says, "I may not have had great business experience, but I knew that if the employees didn't show up, if they didn't get the product in the bucket and shipped out, we didn't have a business. I learned that by watching my father over the years, by gaining an understanding that the leader's main job is nurturing the people."

As Leslie established good relationships with the employees, she began to see other behaviors and practices that she judged unethical and detrimental to the future of the company.

She observed that the president's relationship with the company's vendors was not only adversarial but confrontational. She began to attend vendor meetings and watched as the president killed several deals that, in her words, "would have been great deals. But he was trying to get one or two pennies more out of the vendor. I'd heard that our vendors felt intimidated just calling on us. This is not how I wanted to do business."

Somehow Leslie knew instinctively that, just as leaders and top managers must respect their customers, colleagues, and employees, they must also respect their vendors.

Finally, the pressure built up enough that she could no longer tolerate her relationship with the president. She told him, "Look, I think we should change the way we're doing things. I don't think we should play these pricing games with our vendors. So let's not talk about cutting a penny here and there, let's talk about how we can create a new, better relationship. We may want to go with this particular vendor because of all the other aspects of who they are with service, integrity, quality. It's not just about money, and it's not at all about wheeling and dealing. We depend on these people."

The changes Leslie was bringing about in culture, in relationships with employees and vendors, made John very uncomfortable. All of it represented to him an enormous loss of control, and like too many managers he was driven so much by his ego that he was unable to let go of what he perceived to be his "control." Being dictatorial with employees meant he didn't have to reach out personally and could hide his own potential vulnerabilities behind the mask of control. Pushing vendors for another penny or nickel on price meant he focused those relationships on nothing but numbers and could remain aloof from personal contact and connection.

To John, success in management was built on old concepts of command and control, whereas to Leslie success in management was built on community and collegiality.

The arrangement of John as president and Leslie as asset manager was probably unwieldy and unworkable to begin with, and it finally got to the point that it could not continue without a severe detrimental effect on employee morale and company progress.

As time passed, Leslie clearly emerged as the senior executive in the company and began to face the ethical question of how to resolve the situation with John. Here was a man her father had known for years and had hired into the job. She wanted to be respectful to him, but more and more she struggled with how to do that while fulfilling her responsibility as asset manager for the family. Plus, how could she reinstitute the supportive leadership style of her father and at the same time ensure that the company continued to meet its commitments and grow?

This was the almost classic question of "When does the well-being of one person begin to impose on the well-being of the group? When does doing the right thing for the good of the enterprise require doing something very detrimental to an individual?" Even with her criticisms of his management style and with their sometimes sharp differences, she understandably did not want to see him go through the embarrassment and inevitable loss of self-esteem that comes with being fired.

It is far too common for managers to avoid this hard choice, and they do it in several ways. They may create a new job for the person, one that gets him or her out of the way but still on the payroll. They may try to "reorganize" so that the person can maintain the office, the title, and the salary while doing some menial busywork. Or they may try to get someone else from another company, or if in a large company, get someone from another department to hire him or her.

Leslie took the hard choice. She confronted the president and told him he would have to resign; then she worked out a reasonably generous severance agreement with him.

But his leaving did not mean the end of the challenges to Leslie's sense of the right way to do things. There was still much work to do.

She describes her industry as "to some extent like Wild West stuff. In our industry there really weren't any distribution agreements [a document that, like a contract, establishes ground rules and understandings between company and distributor]. There was too much wheeling and dealing to suit me."

Leslie decided that she would insist her company have distribution agreements. Because her industry was not accustomed to them, her salespeople objected strenuously, insisting that this would make their jobs more difficult. They told her it would be giving the distributors another reason to say no. But Leslie persisted.

She explained her philosophy: "This makes sense for both of us, the distributors and the company. I know it's going to be hard, but it makes sense. This is the opportunity for us to understand exactly what the expectations are, how we're going to do business together. If there are problems, let's establish a procedure for solving the problems. It's a win-win."

It's working, but Leslie found it was very hard to do, and especially so for a woman. "For the most part, this is a man's industry," she says. "I've only met two other women owners."

She has learned that she doesn't have to compromise her principles but also that she can pick her battles. "I just ignore some of the sweetie, honey stuff. And some of it is generational. There's one older gentleman who always calls me things like honey and hon and sweetheart and little lady. He's a very nice man and I just smile and accept it as his way of complimenting me. Yes, it's kind of patronizing, but I can handle it."

What about the younger guys?

"If I get a lot of crap from, you know, a thirty-five-year-old guy customer, who gets this close, who's been drinking, as a lot of people do at trade show receptions, and tries to wrap himself around me, that's a different situation."

She pauses. "We don't need the business that bad."

In fact, if anything characterizes Leslie's approach to business, nothing is worth compromising her basic values of supporting and nurturing her people, being fair with vendors, and being straightforward and honest with customers. And sometimes the choices those values present are not as simple as they seem.

LESSONS TO REMEMBER

- Diagnose the problem thoroughly before you act.
- Take time to learn from people on the front lines.
- Understand that the leader's main job is nurturing the people.

FIX THE MANAGEMENT PROBLEM OR PROTECT YOUR SOCIAL STANDING?

So this key person has known you since you were in
school. So this is a small town and there will be talk. So
what?

THERE'S AN OLD question within the American business world: "Would you rather be a little fish in a big pond or a big fish in a little pond?" Not an easy question.

The little fish doesn't enjoy as much attention and esteem within the large community but also is able to work in relative anonymity.

The big fish gets plenty of attention and esteem within the small community, plus plenty of often unwelcome advice from colleagues at the club, friends at church, and even from the local press, who always keep a probing eye on the big fish. And when the time comes to make a decision that is sure to offend some substantial segment of the small community, the social pressures are enormous.

When Charles Purves (not his real name), with his law degree, an MBA from a prestigious university, and two years with a major financial services firm, returned to his hometown as president of a very large publicly held company that his great-uncle had founded, he was still in his thirties. If people in this small city in the Southwest or officers in the company had doubts about his qualifications or ability, they did not voice them.

The community welcomed him as the honored son of a prominent family, the son from whom everyone had always expected great things.

So it was in the comfort of family and community that Charles went to work. The world had changed since the days of his great-uncle, and the fact of public ownership imposed, as it always does, a set of disciplines and requirements earlier generations had not had to face.

In assessing the landscape of the business, Charles discovered a big problem. Some years before, in the days when companies were "diversifying" rather than sticking to their core businesses, the company had acquired a regional chain of what his older predecessors would have called "lumberyards" but were now called building supply dealers. Like many other similar businesses, the chain was being squeezed hard on one side by large discounters and on the other by small "custom" operators. One was taking the high-volume, low-margin business; the other was taking the low-volume, high-margin business.

The result was an operation going south in a hurry, losing money every quarter, and requiring large infusions of cash from the core company.

Charles called in the building supply company's chief executive, Raymond, a fifty-year-old man who was a well-established and substantial member of the community, a supporter of education, the arts, and various charities. Raymond had known Charles all his life, and while Charles admits it is speculation on his part, "This man probably resented being called in by this kid to explain the problems and possibilities of the business, a business he had been running for several years."

The conversation did not go well. It became clear to Charles that Raymond planned no changes of strategy, that he felt the business was simply in a down cycle and that he could just stick with some of the changes and upgrades he'd made a couple of years before.

In the months after their meeting, the business continued to slide, and in subsequent meetings, Raymond offered no prospect of new strategy or change of any kind. He was resistant to seeking help from outside his operation, including from management consultants or strategic-planning firms, and he was particularly resistant to suggestions from Charles. Raymond's vision had worked in the past and he felt things would "turn around." They always had.

Meanwhile, the lack of performance by the building supply business was becoming a major distraction for Charles and his management team. There seemed no alternative but to make a major change in management.

This kind of decision is always difficult, but Charles's choice went beyond difficult. It was sticky. There was the business, of course, and that part of the equation was easy. Business down, management unresponsive, thus replace management. Done. But not so fast in a small city, where such a high-visibility change creates a ripple effect that can quickly become a tsunami of discontent, bitterness, and community discord. Colleagues can turn against each other; neighbors can become distant; children can be told not to associate with certain other children.

Charles was aware of these possibilities, plus there was the real concern that the building supply business itself might lose some large commercial customers if a substantial number of people allied themselves with the man who had been fired.

But Charles's overriding obligation was his fiduciary responsibility to his stockholders as well as his feeling of responsibility for the very large number of employees who would lose their jobs if the business failed. So he offered Raymond what he felt was an appropriate severance package and asked for his resignation.

"I caught a lot of flack about it," Charles recalls, "and it was exacerbated by the fact that I decided to do a national search for a new chief executive, which meant I'd be bringing in a person from out of town rather than promoting someone into the job."

Charles was more concerned about the social impact on his family than on himself. "My wife caught a lot of grief in the community, and even my kids were hassled about it by other kids at school."

Charles's next hard choice was legal. Raymond wanted to negotiate the severance settlement and hired a lawyer who, of course, was also quite well known in the community. He called Charles one day and laid out a series of demands.

"He asked for crazy stuff, an amount of money that was neither reasonable nor fair. But the issue was, 'Do I pay this and just make this go away, avoid further publicity, avoid any more harassment for myself, my family, and the company, or do I stick to my guns?' I decided to stand up to him. I told him I thought he was being outrageous and completely wrong. Later on, he backed down."

There are executives who would have handled this differently. For instance, it would have been a reasonably acceptable rationale to pay the money in order to avoid the likelihood of any further negative publicity that might have an impact on customer attitudes. The other side of that issue is that paying hush money to avoid a lawsuit or negative publicity often invites other legal threats, and there is no way to keep these negotiations and outcomes completely confidential. Regardless of legal agreements, the news gets around that this or that company will pay to stay out of the press. The news also gets around when a company signals that it will not easily settle a potential suit just to make it go away.

For Charles, there were two ethical issues in this situation. One was that in taking the easy way out, just paying off the hush money, he would not be true to himself in achieving a fair result. Second was the fact that Charles was representing the stockholders, and it would not have been good stewardship of their money to make an unreasonable settlement.

Charles knows that others might have made a different decision. "But the way I look at those things," Charles says, "then and now, is that you have to have a strong sense of what is right and what is fair. I was convinced, and others were too, that this change needed to be made. I also felt I could not pay money just to make an unpleasant situation go away. I knew there might be hell to pay publicly, and a lot of hassle associated with it, but it was the right thing to do, and in the end it was the best thing for the business as well as all the other employees."

LESSONS TO REMEMBER

- Disregard social pressure when making tough management decisions.
- Resist the temptation to buy your way out of an unpleasant situation.

TWENTY-ONE

LIVE YOUR FAITH OR GIVE IN TO MARKETPLACE PRESSURE?

Living your faith and managing a business are not necessarily in conflict, but they can be.

THERE HAS BEEN a lot of attention paid recently to the confluence of spirituality and work, and concomitantly there have also been a lot of questions about just how fervently people of a specific faith should bring their religion into the workplace. Of course, a person's values, sense of integrity, and ethical standards may derive from his or her faith, but when does taking one's faith to work become proselytizing rather than simply exemplary living?

Jack Herschend's life and work provide some answers and insights into how one person handles that question. Jack is a man of integrity and his integrity is founded on his Christian faith. When he goes to work, he does not leave that faith at home, and in the forty years he was chairman and chief executive officer of Silver Dollar City in Branson, Missouri, he faced plenty of business situations in which his strong sense of right and wrong was challenged and tested.

Consider the business. It's theme parks, it's show business. How in the world does the top person hold true to the Christian principles by which he says the company operates while at the same time confronting and making major strategic decisions about such issues as gambling or serving alcohol, plus handling the daily management challenges of marital infidelity or office romances, and also maintaining relationships with celebrities whose good or bad behavior may reflect on the company?

"There are so many stories," Jack says, "that it's difficult to know which ones to tell. I don't believe I was ever tempted to compromise my standards, but there were plenty of times when I had to defend those standards, even to my own staff."

Asked if he ever did so even when it meant a loss of revenue for the company, he replied, "Oh yes. More than a few times."

The easiest one, he insists, was the commitment to never allow gambling in any Silver Dollar City venue, even though this meant forgoing potentially millions of dollars in revenue and profits. This ban includes not only SDC itself but also the company's other operations and partnerships, including Dollywood in Pigeon Forge, Tennessee, plus attractions in Florida, Georgia, Maryland, Pennsylvania, South Carolina, and Texas, businesses that employ over four thousand people and annually host more than 6.5 million guests. In addition to a concern for the company's position with its own facilities, Jack's brother, Peter, who shares both his faith and his commitment to high ethical standards, has worked diligently against the spread of gambling in their home state of Missouri.

"The proponents call it 'gaming,' " Jack says, "but we call

it what it is, old-fashioned gambling. And we think it's wrong. We think it hurts people least able to afford to lose money, and it undermines all sorts of things we believe in: family, community, and so on. We've put a million and a quarter dollars into the fight, and it's ongoing."

The national gambling trend, everything from state lotteries to slot machines and table games, demonstrates that there is big money to be made. Jack insists that it was never a consideration, that it was never proposed and never discussed. "We didn't even calculate the possibilities."

A more complex and difficult situation has to do with the consumption of alcoholic beverages. For Jack, the story is intensely personal. "My father divorced my mom when I was eight, but I was old enough to witness the huge negative impact that alcoholism had on him and on our family. It's something I'll always remember, and yes, I've let those experiences profoundly impact the company's policies.

"Understand that we used to sell beer in the Silver Dollar City campground. Things went along pretty good, I guess, but then there began to be some pressure about hard liquor and whether we ought to serve it for groups that ask for it. Of course, because of my personal experience, I was bothered that we even sold beer.

"So I went to my brother and said, 'Pete, I know you're a good Episcopalian and this doesn't bother you a bit, but it's giving me heartburn. I admit it's personal, but I just have this vivid memory of how painful my childhood was and alcohol was at the center.' "

"Pete said, 'No big deal. Let's get rid of it.' So we decided against both the hard liquor and the beer. We took the beer out of the campground."

Did that decision sacrifice revenue and profits? "I'm not really sure how much," Jack says, "but clearly a lot of other outfits make a lot of money on alcohol."

A big advantage for Jack and his brother is that Silver Dollar City is a privately held company and they can set whatever policies they wish as long as the other stockholders agree. But when even a privately held company reaches out from its self-contained status and takes on a partner, the decisions become far more complex and the ethical issues take on an expanded concern. For instance, how ethical is it to insist that your partner sacrifice profit in order to meet your ethical concerns that he may not share?

Once again, the alcohol question reared its head, this time in the context of a partnership, and as is so often the case, questions of ethicality are never as cut and dried as one would like them to be. One person's standards of integrity can be seen by another person as overly restrictive barriers to doing business.

The company is now in business in Stone Mountain, Georgia, a major attraction, and has partnered with Marriott to operate two hotels there. Of course, Marriott serves alcohol. Jack is no longer in active management of the company, but he still sits on the board and his voice is very influential. While the situation with Marriott is not likely to change at this point, it still bothers him.

Jack again went to his brother Pete and said, "We're hypocrites. We serve alcohol there, we don't serve it here. This troubles me and we need to do something."

So Jack and Pete presented a position to the stockholders and board, proposing that the company's policy from now on should be against serving alcohol.

"I gave my personal background to explain the genesis of the anti-alcohol policy. The advantages of it seem so clear you don't have to explain it in detail. The disadvantage, of course, is that it will severely limit our ability to do future partnerships with people like Marriott."

If Jack were in a more conventional business, the choices might not be so difficult and his ability to imbue all the participants with his own well-defined ethical standard might be less challenging. But show business is something else altogether. The "employees" differ from more conventional employee groups in the degree to which their creative efforts make the difference between profit and loss. Writers, producers, directors, actors, sound and lighting technicians, and others involved in creating shows that attract and entertain the customers are focused on one thing: the entertainment value of what they do.

Which raises the question about content and the risks of offending members of the audience. Aren't entertainers always pushing the envelope of what is acceptable? And when they speak, aren't they in effect representing the company? The answers are yes and yes. Of course, Silver Dollar City's reputation for family entertainment made content concerns less critical than they might be in other entertainment companies. Raunchy, vulgar jokes and situations were not likely even to be suggested to the SDC show producers.

"Still," Jack says, "entertainers thrive on laughs and applause, and sometimes they'll cross the line to get it."

So how do you deal with it without becoming a daily censor? Jack's approach was to establish expectations that could be shared by the staff, so that they and not he would set the standards. But it was a costly lesson to teach; it came as a result of another of those hard choices between profit and integrity.

"It happened several years ago," Jack remembers. "We had a show we were going to do at Echo Hollow [one of the show venues] in front of four thousand people. And this particular show was the entire market hook for the year, running from Memorial Day through Labor Day—a huge investment for us.

"I can't overly stress how big a deal it was for us. It was high profile, featured on our television commercials and in other marketing efforts. It was written by a top person."

There were a lot of staff people involved in preparing the show, and Jack himself read the script.

"But I missed something important," he explains. "I just didn't pick up on the fact that the lead part, a pastor, was being made out to be a ridiculous buffoon until I actually saw the show onstage. I can laugh like the next guy, but this seemed nasty, unnecessarily ridiculing this pastor. It gave me a sick feeling in the pit of my stomach."

What to do? "I called the entertainment director to get his read. Of course he thought the show was wonderful; in fact, as you might suspect, all the folks who were in on the birthing of the show thought it was wonderful. I decided they just couldn't be objective, so I overruled them all and shut down the show."

By any measure, this is an extreme action by a chief executive. The risk is that it communicates a lack of confidence and trust in the people responsible for the product; thus it can have a profoundly negative impact on morale.

And it did. There was great resistance from the marketing and operations people. They accused Jack of wearing his faith on his sleeve and being unduly restrictive in his interpretation of the show. They called it overkill.

Then there was the financial impact. "It took three weeks to rewrite and reopen the show. It was very expensive and very painful." Jack pauses. "But it was worth it because the message that was sent throughout the organization had a ripple effect that has lasted years and years. Up until that time, I felt like the resident policeman. I'd have to go to all the shows, but after this episode, I no longer had to. It was just so clear what the organization stood for that it has had a tremendous long-term benefit. I never had to worry about it again."

It's tempting to believe that in a company that characterizes itself as a "Christian company" and that tries to maintain standards of operations and behavior based on that faith, there might not be some of the situations that plague other organizations. Marital infidelity and office romances, for instance.

"Oh, I suspect we have most if not all the situations that every other company has, even infidelity and love affairs."

So, are they handled any differently? In most companies, concerns about office romances have to do with their impact on morale and productivity. As long as those are not affected and as long as sexual harassment is not involved, some companies choose to ignore the personal affairs of their employees. Others prohibit romances under any circumstances, and summarily fire the participants.

"Our approach had generally been a stern disapproval and termination," says Jack. "We felt it was a matter of the signal it sends and the morale problems it creates. That had always been our position until the situation I'm about to tell you now."

At Silver Dollar City, the procedure for terminating an employee is to get approval from the next higher authority. In keeping with that, one of Jack's top people came in one day and told him about a key person who was having an affair with another person in the company.

"We can't tolerate that," the manager told Jack, "so I want your approval to terminate him."

Jack would normally have endorsed the action for the good of the organization, but this day was different from other days. The situation Jack found himself in illustrates how faith considerations can make you uncomfortable with how you've always done things, particularly when the livelihood of employees is as stake. What may have always seemed the right thing to do can look different in light of a new understanding or a new revelation that comes at just the critical time.

Jack doesn't read the Bible every morning, but on this day he had read the story in the eighth chapter of the Gospel of John concerning Jesus's defense of the woman accused of adultery. (This chapter contains the famous admonition, "If any one among you is without sin, let him be the first to throw a stone . . .")* The coincidence of his morning's reading and the manager's recommendation struck Jack as having great significance. He was sitting there listening to why the employee should be terminated and at the same time thinking of the story from John.

"I said, 'Give me twenty-four hours to think about it.' I'm sure it was confusing to Bill [not his real name], but he'd worked with me a long time, so he knew something was on my mind." Jack went home and thought and prayed about the situation.

The next morning he met with Bill and asked, "Bill, if Jesus Christ was sitting in that chair right over there, would

---

*New International Version Study Bible.

you recommend that we terminate Jerry [not his real name]?" Jack explains, "Bill is a believer, so my question sort of stopped him. He paused a long time and said, 'I don't know, I hadn't thought about it like that.' We ended up giving Jerry a thirty-day probation period without pay with the understanding that the romance would end. The result was that we had a valuable employee for the next fifteen years."

What about the woman?

"Nothing. She was an hourly worker and we didn't take any disciplinary action with her because Jerry was higher in the organization. Certainly she had a role, but our choice was to discipline the person we felt had the greater management responsibility."

The risk was in the long-term impact of this action. Office romances are never a secret, even when the participants believe they're being completely discreet. So what signal did this different way of handling it send to the employees, and how would future situations be handled?

"Believe me," Jack asserts, "we did not send a signal that we condoned this kind of behavior, but the offshoot was that, within our culture, within the very warp and weave of our organization, when we were making a decision concerning people's livelihood, we would make it with the thought that Christ was right there in the room with us."

So while most managers probably would consider that the right thing to do would be to terminate both employees, Jack chose the path of forgiveness rather than judgment. Many organizational theorists would call this a radical solution.

Jack laughs. "Well, Jesus was really a radical, you know."

When asked if this story really answers the question, "How would Jesus fire someone?" Jack responds, "No, it's more than that. I hope all these stories I've shared are about how Jesus would lead a company."

LESSONS TO REMEMBER

- Make decisions that will transmit your values throughout the company.
- Try always to act on the side of compassion.

EXTEND YOURSELF OR
DEFEND YOURSELF?

*When accidents happen, who comes first: the victim's
family or the legal interests of the company?*

THERE IS A wide range of businesses that involve some risk
to the customer as a normal part of the process. Airlines, for
instance, operate with a high degree of safety and maintain
elaborate systems for ensuring safety, from crew training to
maintenance processes, but they also have well-established
emergency response procedures because they are intensely
aware that nothing ensures immunity from accidents.

In the outdoor recreation business, from white-water raft-
ing to skiing to rock climbing to horseback riding and even to
relatively benign activities such as guided walking and bicy-
cling vacations, there is always the possibility that a customer
will be injured or killed. These businesses, too, have response
procedures in case of accident.

It may or may not be true that the managers of these businesses care deeply about the safety of their customers, but it's
definitely true that the prescribed response procedures are

designed to protect the companies from lawsuits as well as to help the loved ones of those killed or injured.

Put yourself in this position: If you were the senior executive of a company and had just been notified that one of your customers was killed in an accident, what would your priorities be? Would you adopt the complete institutional response, making sure that the company's rear was covered legally, or would you respond with humanity and support for the people most personally affected, regardless of the possible impact on future legal action? If you decided to do both—and this is the decision most people would probably make—how would you do it? How would you balance your inclinations as a caring human being with your obligations as a manager and steward of the company's best interests?

This was the choice that John Gans found himself facing after only eight months as executive director of the National Outdoor Leadership School. John was on a business trip when he received an emergency call that a young woman in one of the NOLS outdoors skills courses, Katie B., had died in a river-crossing exercise.

"I had been with the school before then," John recalls, "but I was new to this position. One thing I had learned is that you are always aware that something like this can happen, and it makes the job different from a lot of other leadership positions. The school's outcomes are usually phenomenally positive, and our safety record is exemplary, but you know there is always that remote possibility of a truly tragic outcome."

Because the student teams are in remote wilderness areas for their courses, the school, like other companies in higher-risk situations, had a system for communicating emergency information. In this case, as John recalls, the field instructors made a ground-to-air call by radio; an airliner received the call and, in turn, notified air traffic control in Salt Lake City. The school had a code system, so that when the message was received, the school personnel knew immediately that there had been a fatality, the course it occurred on, and the location. That's when they made the initial call to John.

Upon hearing the news, John traveled all night to return to the school's headquarters. His operations manager had made an initial call to the girl's family, told them there had been an accident and that she had died. At that point, the family cut off the conversation. There had been no further contact.

Now the situation was in John's hands.

The list of constituents with whom John needed to communicate was daunting: the insurance company, the lawyers, the school's staff members, student groups in the field, the board of trustees, and, most important, the family. "Being the focal point of so much pressure," John recalls, "is something you just can't prepare yourself for. All the parties have diverse interests. The board is trying to protect the reputation of the school; the insurance company is trying to reduce the financial exposure; and the attorneys are trying to limit the possible legal problems. And of course, the family is dealing with the most horrible crisis any family could possibly deal with.

"There are certain protocols, of course, and you turn to them, but they can't prepare you for the many questions you have to face," he says. "The first issue is information. You have to gather all the information you can to determine as accurately as possible what happened. And the essence of the ethical questions that ran through the situation was, 'How open are you with the information, specifically, how open are you with the family?'

"My nature is to be as open as possible. I feel that if you're open, in the end it's the best thing to do. And so my inclination in those early days after the accident was to provide as much information to the family as I could."

The information must serve many purposes, and some of them are not so obvious immediately. "One of the first things is to make sure that this situation does not signal an operational weakness or procedure we need to change or deal with in order to make the program better if necessary. Then the legal people are going to want the information, as is the insurance company. They, of course, are in the mode of protecting the school."

But what about the family? How much information should they receive? It is around this question that John made the first hard choice in balancing the family's interests and the school's interests, which may not be the same.

"It's fair to say that the insurance company's position would be to withhold information and release as little as possible. That's understandable, because there's a huge number of concerns in a situation like this. The school could even be put at risk. You could have a lawsuit that could go beyond your insurance deductible and literally bankrupt the organization.

"Or there could be publicity that would discourage any new students from signing up. We could have our permits pulled by the land management agency, an action which, since we don't own classrooms, would end our access to the public lands."

While John had established contact with the girl's aunt, there had been no communication with the parents since the initial notification. "I felt we needed to remedy that, so I offered through the aunt to have family members come to Lander [Wyoming] at our expense. I said we would release information as we knew it. In addition, I committed to have an independent external review of the incident that we would share with them. This was not something the insurance company was comfortable with, but in the end we got their reluctant blessing."

The aunt's response to John's invitation was that the family did not want a direct family member to make the trip but preferred to have the father's closest friend be there when Katie's fellow students came in from the field. The friend was also a lawyer.

"This was clearly not the person we had invited, and this was not the tone of what we wanted. What complicated the situation was that the father's friend was also the parent of a NOLS graduate, and both he and his son, a close friend of Katie's, were planning to come. So we had an extensive debate among staff and finally issued the invitation. Not only that, we gave them access to the staff debriefing when the group came in from the field and gave them opportunities to ask questions of the staff and students."

It turned out that much of the new information was being heard at the same time by school staff and the father's friend. By any measure, this is an extraordinary degree of openness in the face of possibly severe legal consequences. Still, despite what some might define as legally risky, John wanted to reach out even more to the family.

"I conveyed to the family that I and other representatives of the school would be interested in attending any memorial service or funeral. We were initially rebuffed and told that wouldn't be appropriate, but for some reason something changed and we were told it would be okay for us to attend the memorial. Although we'd passed along our willingness to meet with the family, to bring maps, and give them all the information we had at the time, there was no invitation for anything beyond attending the service."

John invited his board chairman and a key employee to accompany him to the service, but before leaving there was still one decision to make. A follow-up team had visited the site of the accident and had been instructed to try to find Katie's lost backpack because John wanted to return her personal effects to the family.

John remembers getting the recovered pack just before he was to leave for the memorial service. As he was repackaging Katie's effects for delivery, he came across two items that gave him pause. The first was her journal.

"I realized that what she had written could either help the school or harm the school or both."

How so?

"It could give us another view of the incident and perhaps help us see a way to prevent a future accident. It could also paint a quite negative picture. When these students are in the midst of a course, they are outside their normal comfort zones. That's just part of the experience. We're well aware that any student's journal is probably going to remark heavily on how tired they are, how challenging it is, how difficult it was. There are up and down days, and a lot of the journal is going to reflect on the difficulties. Any student's journal can make it sound as if the experience is over the student's head. We were well aware that a typical student's journal could make it sound to Katie's parents as if she was not fully comfortable with the experience."

John and his people felt they had to read the journal, not to censor it or to probe Katie's personal feelings, but to learn as much as they could about everything concerned with the accident. It would have been easy to hold on to the journal because technically there was no requirement to release it. In fact, the family didn't even know a journal existed.

So, was there an internal discussion about whether to release it to the family?

"We discussed it, though not with the insurance company, but there was no great internal debate. Even though we knew there could be mixed conclusions, we all felt the right thing to do was to deliver Katie's journal to her family. So we did."

The second item that gave John pause was a NOLS coffee mug that Katie had bought and taken to the field with her. "It clearly was a personal effect," John says, "but I looked at it with the big NOLS logo on it and thought, 'I can't deliver this.' I don't know if I thought it would be too much of a reminder for the family or if it was just something going on inside me. It just didn't feel right to me. I wasn't ready to throw it away, though, so I put the mug on my desk, put everything else in the bag, and took off for the airport."

After the memorial service, John, the board chairman, and the employee returned to the hotel. But John felt a further dilemma, one that tugged at his sense of how he should be and what he should do. He felt strongly that he wanted to make a deeper contact with the family. This was partly for himself and partly to demonstrate a sincere concern that went beyond his role as head of the school. "But we hadn't been invited to the house or anything. So here we are with another question of 'Well, do we call it a night and fly home? We've signed the guest book, so should we leave?' It was one of those cases in which it was very difficult to maintain openness with the family, yet I felt the need to do so. I decided to telephone the home and ask if there was a chance that we could stop by the next morning."

John talked with the aunt, who talked with Faye, Katie's

mother, who then invited John's group over that evening. "So suddenly we go from not getting any information to being invited into the midst of a family gathering."

Soon after John walked in the front door, his sympathy and concern deepened into shock as he realized the extent of the family's loss. John had been naturally moved by the tragedy itself, the horror of a child's death, but in the home he was confronted with an almost overwhelming sense of tragedy: Katie's father, Bill, was bedridden at the time, suffering from multiple sclerosis and complications of recent surgery. Her mother, Faye, was in remission from breast cancer after a long and debilitating bout. Katie's younger brother, Jack, had a recent history of behavioral difficulties that were now exacerbated by Katie's death.

John realized that Katie had become a primary physical and emotional support for her father. Bill was still working in a job that required some travel, but his disability prevented him from doing it alone. He needed Katie as both caregiver and companion.

All this had been revealed in conversations with various family members—uncles, aunts, others—throughout the evening. John learned also that Bill was an engineer and an outdoor enthusiast who had wanted Katie to go on the fateful trip.

At the end of the evening, John offered to Bill and Faye that he would like to stop by the next day and talk about what happened. Bill was a believer in the power of the wilderness experience, so he was very interested in what happened. Faye was less so but agreed to the visit.

The next morning, John sat at Bill's hospital bed for about three hours. "It was a very powerful time together," John recalls with some sadness. "He had a lot of questions and understood everything we were going through. He understood topographic maps and elevation and rivers. He understood pretty much everything.

"The meeting with Faye was different. She pulled out a large envelope in which she had saved an eight-by-ten photograph of Katie from every year of her schooling. She just spread them out across the bed and talked about how Katie was all she had to hang on to during her bout with cancer.

"It was so dramatically clear that Katie had been the rock in the family. She was everything. I hadn't realized the role she played in the family. I began to go back and forth between Faye and Bill. Bill wanted very much to talk about the details of the accident, and Faye just wanted to talk about who Katie was and what she meant to them."

Meanwhile, the chairman of the board, who had been mostly in the role of observer, became convinced that there would be a lawsuit. He mentioned it to John, who felt the time was not right to discuss it. "I just remember thinking over and over again, it just doesn't matter. This is not the thing you think about right now. A lawsuit was the furthest thing from my mind, even though at some level I knew I'd have to deal with it, but not now, not in this environment.

"I still recall to this day holding Bill's hand that day. I held it the whole time we talked. I was holding it as we got closer in the conversation to the time of Katie's getting in the river and being swept down, and then the unknown period of time before she drowned. I recall the seconds of describing it and the holding of the hand and watching the dynamics of what was happening. And all the while I was looking intimately into his eyes. There was not one time our eyes wavered from each other. I'll never forget that. I recall so powerfully being almost a unified whole. I have no recollection of what else was going on, other than Bill and myself.

"It was one of the most powerful experiences of my life, and yet I almost feel guilty saying that."

This experience convinced John he had made the right decision in sharing information with the family, even after being rebuffed by them. "In a way," he says, "you could say we were forcing ourselves on them, but we stayed the course because I truly felt it was the right thing to do."

John and Bill stayed in touch via e-mail during the following weeks. John provided more information as it became available from the team investigating the accident. Then suddenly, communication from the family stopped, and John received word that the family was considering its options and further communication was not appropriate. The clear implication was that things were moving toward a lawsuit.

"I was not surprised," recalls John, "particularly given Katie's role in that family."

But as any executive who has been involved in legal action will realize, this development changed the dynamic of whatever personal connection there might have been with the family. John's options would by necessity be constrained by legal considerations.

For instance, he felt the final accident report as reviewed and edited by the insurance company and attorneys was deficient. But he also knew that his responsibility for the stewardship of the school required that he recognize and appreciate the insurance company's point of view and its expanding role as the reality of a lawsuit become more probable.

"There was no dishonest information being presented in

the report, but I felt their desire to cross out or skip over parts was not in line with what I personally felt. I lobbied to be as open as possible because I didn't feel that glossing over any of this stuff was going to work. Besides, I knew there was a very savvy, smart party on the other side and they'd see through all of it."

In a subsequent meeting with Bill and his attorney, John's concerns about the report were realized. After reading it thoroughly, Bill became very angry and said the report was too sanitized.

"I must admit I agreed with him, but at this point other parties have control over the process. From the viewpoint of the school, that's not all wrong. The other parties have an important role to play."

The lawsuit was filed, and both parties agreed to try mediation. It happened that the night before the mediation meeting John and his people stayed at the same hotel as Bill. At breakfast the next morning, John heard Bill yell across the dining room, "I won't be satisfied until he's in jail."

John realized that Bill was referring to him. "Those were pretty tough words to hear after what I thought had been a good relationship and, at times, a very intimate one. But in retrospect, they were understandable words as well."

The legal situation was, as many are, debatable as to what the outcome of a suit might have been. NOLS had releases signed by parents and students, plus copies of e-mails from Bill saying how important the wilderness experience is and how much he wanted his daughter to attend.

"We had a choice to make," John says. "There was no smoking gun, no reason to believe we'd lose the case. Nothing said, 'You've got to settle this thing.' My only concern was the family situation."

The mediation lasted less than a day. At the end of it, John approached Bill's lawyers and asked if he could say good-bye to Bill. "They looked at me like I was nuts and said that was not a good idea. I said I'd like to say good-bye if that's all right with Bill. They replied, 'Look, we worked all day on this; think of everything invested in this agreement. Why would you want to risk having it fall apart?' But I persisted and asked that they ask Bill. They agreed to ask him, and Bill agreed to see me."

This was the same day John had heard Bill shout that he wouldn't be satisfied until John was in jail. Still, John was not willing to let the communication end with a formal legal agreement.

"So I go in and I say good-bye to Bill and thank him for the exchange that we had when we were communicating. And he breaks down crying and reaches forward and grabs my hand. Then we hug and he says, 'John Gans, you're a good man and I want you to know I had to do this for my family. You've been up-front with me the whole way. I thank you.' "

It is very difficult for people to maintain their empathy and their sense of integrity in the midst of legally threatening situations, and who knows whether doing that will make a difference from an organizational point of view? It will, however, make a difference for the people themselves.

There is a postscript to this story. Years later, after both Faye and Bill had died, John received a call via satellite phone from one of his course leaders in Alaska. On the first night of a four-week wilderness trip similar to the one on which Katie had died, the group was doing its usual orientation with every student telling how he or she first heard about NOLS. One of the students was a man named Jackson who said, "Well, I heard about NOLS from my sister, who died on a course several years ago." This was the last surviving member of Katie's family, her younger brother Jack—now Jackson—who'd had such behavior problems those years before. He has now completed two NOLS courses and is a strong believer in the school and its purpose.

As John tells this story, he is sitting at his desk and drinking coffee from the NOLS mug he took from Katie's backpack.

"It's a reminder," he says, "that the decisions you make every single day have a powerful impact in so many ways. It's a reminder that there will be days that shake you to the core, days that require a different kind of leadership. It's a reminder to me of the purpose, the values, and the importance of all our decisions. And so it moves."

LESSONS TO REMEMBER

- Don't let the fear of a lawsuit trump your basic humanity.
- Trust the power of a personal connection even in times of conflict.
- Go beyond what anyone would expect in order to demonstrate your willingness to help others.
- Always give people the information they deserve to have.

TWENTY-THREE

CHOICES THE AUTHORS MADE

Authors James Autry and Peter Roy share stories from their own experience. Autry's was a quick choice; Roy's took years.

AUTRY'S HARD CHOICE

My pet peeve has long been against thoughtless, repressive, and silly policies. Every organization has them. Some policies are necessary, of course, but generally speaking there are way too many policies in every organization, and management, in enforcing policies, usually doesn't make an effort to differentiate between the good ones and the silly ones. All are policies, so all are enforced.

My belief is that policies should be enabling and empowering documents, not instruments of restriction and punishment. Before any personnel policy is adopted, I think two questions should be asked: (1) Will this policy repress or liberate the human spirit of our employees? (2) Will this policy get in the way of doing the right thing?

In consulting for several companies over the past fifteen years, I've learned that one of the first things to examine is the personnel policies. Let me put that another way: I want to see the policies that are intended to control behavior, not the ones that establish procedure or process or the ones having to do with financial reporting or record-keeping.

I want to look at the ones that a policy-writer, at one time or another, thought were needed to ensure that all employees behave in a certain way. Some policies may have to do with attendance requirements, with sick leave, or with family leave. There may be policies about dress or office decorum or alcohol on premises or use of the phone or e-mail. And so on. Those are the ones that interest me because, inevitably, there will be policies that prohibit everyone from doing what only a few people are going to do, and usually they'll do it anyway. Those are the silly policies.

I also look for policies that reflect obsolete or inappropriate cultural or societal attitudes. If I find them, I work with my clients to reexamine them and, often, to eliminate them. Another thing: I ask questions about "unwritten policies" and I usually identify some.

My sensitivity to policies came about over thirty years ago, when I was editor in chief of *Better Homes and Gardens* magazine. I had not been in the job long and was faced with the rather daunting task of redesigning and redirecting the magazine's editorial approach. The newsstand sales were in decline, and the advertising market was very competitive, so there was considerable pressure to turn the magazine around.

One area I judged to be weak editorially was interior design. I knew I had to hire a new editorial head of the department, and I knew he or she should be a highly talented designer and manager, as well as someone with credibility in the design community.

I had become very impressed by the editorial coverage of interior design in another magazine, even though there were just a few pages a year devoted to the subject. I knew the department head by reputation, and thought that he just might consider a job that would offer him more pages and a bigger budget for editorial development. The only problem could be a reluctance to move from his home base in New York to *Better Homes and Gardens'* home base in Des Moines, Iowa. This reluctance was a recurring problem in recruiting editors and designers for the magazine.

But I plunged ahead and gave him a call. He was interested, so we began the process of discussing the job, outlining specific duties and expectations, negotiating salary, and so on. I arranged for him to visit Des Moines.

I was impressed with his ideas for improving the interior design editorial as well as with his knowledge about the market and its products. He also seemed to be focused on the need to make design not only attractive but also affordable for our middle-class readers.

I offered him the job.

When he returned to New York, he phoned. "I know you said you'd pay my moving expenses," he said, "but will you also pay Joe's moving expenses?"

"Who's Joe?" I asked.

"My partner," he answered.

I was confused. Understand that this was the early seventies. I had known and worked with gay men, though at the time we were more likely to say "homosexual" than "gay," but "partner" threw me off. I remember thinking, "I thought I was

hiring an individual editor; I didn't know he had a partner."
Of course, I was thinking business partner; perhaps he had a
design firm I didn't know about.

Then he said, "We've lived together a while and both of us
want him to move with me." He paused. "You don't have to
pay the expenses, and I do want the job, but I thought I'd ask."

I finally got it. Dumb me. He was asking if we could pay
those expenses as we might pay the expenses to move a
spouse. This would not be such a surprise or even a big deal
these days in most large companies, but at the time it was
new. And I was certain it had never been done before in our
company, at least not knowingly.

I was positive that our policy would not cover this situation because I had already asked that the policy be stretched
to move an unmarried heterosexual couple, and this had
caused all kinds of angst and discussion before the policy was
finally reinterpreted to include unmarried couples. It had
been very uncomfortable for me personally, and I did not rel-
ish asking our top human resources person to wade into this
policy again.

But this was not the time to hesitate. I certainly didn't want
to delay the process while I investigated the policy, and I
was sure that if I asked HR the answer would be "No." So I
plunged ahead into what at the time were uncharted waters.
"Of course, we'll move both you and Joe and your household
goods."

Then came the moment of truth. I went to the HR department and told the manager what I'd done. He was shocked
but not necessarily alarmed, and said he'd have to clear it
with his boss, the VP for HR.

I said, "I'm not here for clearance. I've already committed
the company, so this is just to inform you and your depart-

ment." I admit it was an arrogant thing to say, but I didn't want the HR guys to think they'd have veto power over this decision.

What followed was a hot phone call from the VP, then a meeting characterized by anger and red faces. He threatened to rescind the offer of moving expenses and admonished me for not checking with his department first.

I was very nervous. My mouth was dry and my usually dependable voice shook a bit when I spoke. I certainly did not want to make an enemy out of this key corporate officer with whom I'd had a positive if sometimes uneasy relationship. While I held a key editorial job, I was not an officer at the time; thus our relationship was not one of peers but of a senior corporate staff person and a departmental manager.

I explained my rationale in interpreting the policy, and he made clear his feeling that interpretation of policy was not in my job description. I told him that my job was to turn around the number one, key moneymaking product in our company, and that I felt I should be free to do whatever I needed to do, within the bounds of ethicality and legality, to acquire the resources to accomplish that goal.

I also told him that to rescind my offer would embarrass me with this key person. Furthermore, if this editor decided then to turn down the job, the magazine's reputation in the design community and with our advertisers could be damaged. I figured the VP would not want to risk any damage to the magazine's reputation, even if he didn't care about mine.

He decided not to rescind the offer, but then he said, "This is a one-time exception to the policy. I don't want to see this again."

At this point, I felt my own personal moment of truth. The policy as he wanted to interpret it was discriminatory and wrong. Not only that, it was sure at one time or another to work against the best interests of the company. Finally, there was no rational reason not to include same-sex couples in the policy. We had employed gay and lesbian people (I use today's language) for years, even though it wasn't openly discussed. Why would we not give them all the benefits of all other employees?

I answered, "I can't promise that I won't do this again. Not only might this be a barrier to hiring some other talented person in the future, but it's also a bad policy."

He became obviously angry, but only said, "We'll see."

For a while, I worried that this situation was going to come back to haunt me, but that was the end of it. I never heard another word.

And the magazine ended up with a hell of a fine design editor.

ROY'S HARD CHOICE

Outsourcing and layoffs are daily news in our economy, so I realize that many people don't have the luxury I had in deciding to leave my job voluntarily. Still, that did not make it any less of a hard choice when faced with making a decision about whether or not to quit. In my case, it was a job to which I had dedicated my life and into which I had poured all of my creative energy for a decade.

I was president of Whole Foods Market, a company that was (and still is) in the forefront of the entire natural lifestyle movement. By resigning, I would be leaving not only a lot of money, but also the power and status that come with being a top executive in a public company.

My hard choice caused all kinds of stress and angst for me

in 1998. I was no longer having any fun, had lost the passion for my work, and was trying to decide whether it was time to leave my position. There were many issues to consider: some financial, some personal, and some ethical.

Though many could argue, and rightfully so, that my decision to leave was made easier by the fact that I had made some real money through our initial public offering and subsequent stock appreciation, still there is no question that by staying I could have become very wealthy by any standard. True enough, but that did not make the personal or the ethical issues any easier to resolve.

Some background and history are important to fully appreciate the decision I faced and the lessons I learned.

The story begins in 1974, when a small natural foods grocery opened on a corner in uptown New Orleans. Whole Food Company was founded by two friends of mine, Jon Maxwell and Kathleen O'Connor. I was eighteen at the time and had dropped out of college. I was interested in natural and organic foods, and Jon and Kathleen gave me a job. Within four years I was running the business and buying out their interest in the company.

In 1981, I opened one of the first natural foods supermarkets in the country and was at the forefront of this burgeoning movement. By 1988, I was interested in more expansion than I could do on my own and began thinking about joining forces with another company in order to do bigger things. I approached John Mackey and Craig Weller, two of the founders of Whole Foods Market, a very similar company based in Austin, Texas. They had opened very successful stores in Austin and Houston and were also interested in aggressive expansion. We struck a deal to combine our companies. The plan was to seek venture capital and to take the fledgling natural foods supermarket concept nationwide. Amazingly, it was to work beyond our wildest dreams.

The decision to sell was a very hard choice in and of itself. By 1988, I had been CEO of Whole Food Company for ten years. The similarity in our company names was purely coincidental. Ironically, it was the reason I ended up meeting John and Craig in the first place. At one of our first industry trade shows, one of our suppliers hosted a reception and said to me, "Let me introduce you to the guys that ripped off your name." That was our initial meeting and the beginning of our friendship.

In mulling over the decision to sell, one of the biggest hurdles I needed to get over was whether I could again work for anyone else. I had run my own business for a decade, but John was the CEO of Whole Foods Market and would remain so. I would be working with, but also for him. I liked John and most important, I trusted him. That was a critical factor in making my decision. Also, Whole Foods Market's lengthy mission statement, entitled the "Declaration of Inter-Dependence," was also a factor. It laid out the values and guiding principles of the company and how it was to be managed. I wholeheartedly agreed with the spirit and the intent. It helped me decide I could in fact work with such a company and with John and Craig.

In 1988, upon consummating the deal, I moved my family to California, along with Craig and his family, to expand Whole Foods Market into the motherland of natural and organic foods. We opened our first California location in Palo Alto in January 1989. It was a very exciting and heady time. I grew to know Craig as a man of the highest integrity and work ethic who personified the company's mission statement. I felt confident I had made the right choice and worked as hard as I could to see the company become successful and to bring its core values to bear on how we ran the business.

At its essence, the mission statement articulated a team approach to running the business. There would be little hierarchy, and each store would be organized into largely autonomous teams that made the decisions that affected their workplace quality of life. Hiring, firing, scheduling were all handled at a team level, with little management oversight. The belief was that if decisions were made as close to the customers as possible, team members (the company's term for employees) would feel empowered and be happier—thus customer service would be far better than in a conventional hierarchical structure. People newly hired had to try out for the team and were actually voted on by team members before they received full team member status. Pay raises were even decided at a team level.

All financial information was shared throughout the organization, even to the point of sharing individual salaries. There was a salary cap in place limiting the pay of anyone in the company to eight times the average team member salary (it was later raised to fourteen times). There were egalitarian underpinnings through our handbook, our rhetoric, and largely our practice. We were "in it together" and talked a lot about a "shared fate." Whether we did well or poorly as a team, everyone was to be treated fairly and equitably.

This unique approach helped us successfully stave off strong efforts to unionize our employees in California. In the early 1990s we were the largest nonunion operator of supermarkets in the Bay Area. When we opened our store in Berkeley, the local retail clerks' union, as well as the meat cutters' union, picketed our store for over a year and a half and spent hundreds of thousands of dollars running a corporate smear campaign. I was the first line of defense against this attack and persevered largely because I believed in our mission statement. We ultimately won the battle against the union, and the Berkeley store became one of the most successful stores in the company at that time.

Whole Foods grew rapidly through opening new stores and acquiring others. We had our struggles learning to manage extraordinary growth while overcoming a bumpy start in California and the fierce organizational efforts by the local unions.

Around the same time, we acquired Wellspring Grocery in North Carolina. With stores now on both coasts, in Texas and Louisiana, we marketed ourselves to Wall Street as a national company and were successful in taking the company public in 1992. Our timing was perfect, the IPO was hugely successful, and we were on our way. Shortly after the IPO, I was promoted to president of the company and moved to Austin to work closely with John in managing what was fast becoming a very large company.

Over the course of the next eight years we grew from operating seven stores in four states and doing about $100 million in sales to breaking the $1 billion sales level and operating one hundred stores in twenty states. It was quite a journey.

Even at the highest level of the company, we operated very much as a team. We had monthly executive team meetings at which we hashed out many of the decisions about the direction of the business. It was a very process-oriented way to manage the company, but one that I found stimulating, interesting, and empowering. I believed in what we were doing wholeheartedly, and this gave me the energy to keep getting on the airplanes and dealing with the demands of a stressful job. I was having a lot of fun and the job did not feel like work.

Then, in 1998, things began to change for me. It seemed as if on every level my life was becoming unsettled. At work, John and I began to have conflict. All partnerships have conflict at times, but we began to fundamentally disagree on some important issues about which we both felt strongly. It was divisive for us and for those close to us.

Outside of work, I was also experiencing upheaval. In the summer of 1998, my father died unexpectedly. We had been very close and his death impacted me in many ways, some I did not expect. There was the obvious grief and loss of a loved one, but in addition my dad was a very good friend to me, as well as the person who, more than anyone else, had influenced who I was. Surprisingly though, after his passing, I also experienced a strong sense of liberation. This was totally unexpected. I had the sense that I no longer had to live my life in a way my father would approve. Even though I was not conscious of doing so until after his death, I now realized all of the ways in which I had been seeking his approval. Once he was gone, I felt a new freedom to make some different choices.

At this time, I was also concerned about my health, a concern that became intensified by a particularly alarming episode. I was on my way into Manhattan for what seemed liked the hundredth meeting with a new research analyst to discuss Whole Foods. I was good at investor relations and had enjoyed it the first few years, but in this case I knew I was going to face a young MBA fresh from Harvard or Wharton to answer the same inane questions that I had answered hundreds of times before.

I was dreading the meeting and started wondering how

much longer I could do this. My physician had recently warned me that I had too much stress in my life, and considering other risk factors, he felt I could develop serious heart problems. Then, while heading into New York for this meeting, I was gripped by sharp chest pains. I thought for a moment I could be having a heart attack and had the cell phone in my hand to dial 911.

I calmed myself down and in a few minutes realized it was just anxiety, but it was not a good sign. When I returned home the following day and recounted the experience to my wife, she burst into tears and asked me, "How much longer are you going to keep doing this? Is it really worth it?" The pace and the travel required of my job were wearing me down.

Yet another life-changing event at that time was the departure of our youngest daughter, who was leaving home to go to college. After having our family life totally focused on raising two girls for the past twenty years, I realized my wife and I were facing a major adjustment as well. We had the opportunity and the freedom to re-create our lives together in a different way.

The winds of change seemed to be blowing at me from every direction. So for the first time, I began to seriously question if it was time for me to leave Whole Foods and do something else. What? I was not at all sure. I had always thought of Whole Foods as "my life's work," but now I began to imagine about what more I could do if I could find the courage to walk away.

It was both frightening and stimulating. I did not have enough money to retire, but I would be able to take some time to figure out my next move. Part of me was definitely afraid of giving up the security of the big job, the big earning potential, and the trappings of the title, even though it was clear I was no longer having any fun and had lost the passion for the work.

There was also an ethical issue I was struggling with. There were people in the leadership of the company who were very loyal to me. They looked to me to provide leadership, guidance, and support. I was the champion for their issues as well as my own. Company politics being what they were, I knew that my departure would likely have a negative impact on their futures. This weighed heavily on me. Part of me felt that by leaving I would be abandoning them and this was not the "right" thing to do.

I sought counsel from a few close friends and found it helpful to talk out the issues and just to be heard. One friend shared a metaphor that was very helpful. He talked about the need to repot growing plants. He encouraged me to see my life as a plant that had become restricted and to envision the possibilities if I "repotted my plant." Perhaps I could experience new growth only possible if I was willing to take the next step. This was a very powerful image to me and helped me summon the courage to seriously consider leaving.

I also realized that, with my father gone, I could make this decision without being concerned about his approval. He would have never understood my leaving Whole Foods. In his world, it was just not done. I had a fantastic job and was successful; I knew he would have wondered who but a fool would walk away from such a job and career?

After a lot of anxiety and sleepless nights, I resolved that the best thing for me to do was leave. I mustered my courage and began the conversation with John and the Whole Foods board of directors about my leaving the company. They were supportive, and I announced my resignation from the company in October 1998. Over the next few months I helped to ensure a smooth transition inside the company and in the investor community. I was gone by the end of the year.

On the very day that it was announced to the company and the investment community I was stepping aside, I received two phone calls that in short order confirmed that not only had I made the right decision but that there was a great deal of opportunity outside of Whole Foods. The first was from Steve Demos, CEO of White Wave, asking me to join his board and help him build his business. He had just launched a new soy milk called Silk. I readily accepted his offer and joined his board. In five years, Silk would become the most successful natural foods product ever developed, and it is now in over 90 percent of all the supermarkets in the country.

The second call that same day was from Doug Lehrman, one of the founding partners of North Castle Partners, a new private equity fund that was going to focus exclusively on businesses in the healthy living and aging area, asking if I would join the firm as an adviser. This phone call eventually led to a relationship that has been immensely rewarding to me on many levels, and that continues today.

Looking back, I can now say without reservation that leaving Whole Foods was one of the best career decisions I could have ever made. My life on many different levels blossomed. For me, repotting the plant really worked.

The experience also helped me to understand something important about success—specifically, what it is and what it is not. As president of Whole Foods, I was a success by any conventional standard. Yet, I was not happy. I realized that having the title, the money, the recognition, and all the trappings of success did not make me a success. It was only after I left that I began to experience what real success is all about. For me, it was the freedom of choice about what you do in life, the freedom to work at what you want, when you want, and with people you want to work with. Having that freedom made me feel more successful than ever before.

LESSONS TO REMEMBER

- Don't let policies get in the way of doing the right thing.
- Know that leaving is sometimes the best choice in life.

Hard choices aren't about doing, they're about being.

THE AUTHORS HOPE that the stories in this book have accomplished several goals. We hope they have affirmed your own best instincts in facing the choices that you confront daily. We hope they have convinced you that the process of deciding to do the right thing is not about making decision trees, or diagramming the pros and cons in descending order of importance, or consulting case histories in a textbook, but instead is about looking inside your own best self in determining what to do.

This was most evident in the people we interviewed and in those who told their stories. Of the lessons they teach about facing the hard choices, one of the most important is that when all is said and done—when you have reviewed all the policies, collected all the data, consulted with your staff and colleagues—you're on your own. It's up to you alone to do the right thing and, whenever possible, to bring your influence to bear on others to do the right thing.

Another great lesson is one of consistency and dependability. People who work with and for you have to know they can depend on you to treat similar situations similarly, a basic tenet of justice. The paradox is that you must also be willing to reexamine your decisions and, if necessary, change or readjust the way you've done things in the past in order to respond to a new environment or a new set of circumstances.

Making the hard choices always requires commitment and courage. You can't imbue an organization with integrity unless you have the commitment to model ethical behavior every day and unless you have the courage to act out of integrity and on behalf of ethical practices.

Are we the authors saying that effectiveness as a leader is best achieved through adopting an imperative of integrity in all your behavior? Absolutely. We have found that leaders who work to be the kind of people they want to be are, at the same time, the kind of leaders they want to be.

Consider our storytellers. They had to face down authority figures, angry customers, threats to their careers, and in two cases even to their lives. They had to balance their obligations to stockholders and owners, to employees, to customers, to vendors, and to their community, realizing that often these groups have conflicting interests. How did they do that? Only by remaining centered on the things that matter most: their passion for good work and good results, their dedication to fair and equitable treatment for all the people who depend on them, and their abiding belief that acting with integrity is the surest way to succeed in work and in life.

But understand this: It is far easier to be one of the old-fashioned top-down, command-control, power-based bosses who hide behind their positions of authority rather than use them to support their people. They often dismiss issues of ethics and integrity as not being relevant to the "real world."

They see their choices as black-and-white and never in shades of gray. But as you have seen in this book, the real-world hard choices frequently come from rejecting the obvious black-and-white choices and looking deeper into the problem.

Chip Baird (page 169) passed up $50 million in revenue to do what he believed was the right thing for the culture of his company, for its people, and for its future. You can argue with that choice, as many businesspeople might, but you can't argue with Chip's belief that his company would be better off financially in the long term because he demonstrated that his company's foundation of integrity would not yield to short-term financial gain.

Doug Greene (page 31) made much the same kind of risky choice by standing up to a bullying customer. Doug chose to pass up short-term financial advantage for his new company in order to stick to his vision of a business built on fairness and balance.

Let's face it: The hard choices are often about money, and it's always easier to defend a decision you make because of money. The rule to remember is that when it's between money and human values, choose values. Jack Herschend (page 201) sacrificed significant revenues when he shut down a show at Silver Dollar City because he found the content offensive. He reopened the show only after the script was rewritten. Tim Tuff (page 55) shut down a factory, at great financial sacrifice, until he judged it to be running properly and safely.

Understand that this is not about doing, it's about being. There's no shortage of information about what to do. You can find loads of technical data and advice. You can find formats for situation analysis and decision assumptions. In other words, you can find plenty of material that can be useful in making certain decisions and choices, but the authors contend that there is nothing in handbooks or textbooks or policy manuals that can guide you in making the truly hard choices. Those are made only from the heart, not from the head. Those come only from who you are, not from what you do or what position you have.

Unfortunately, we in organizational life have been conditioned to believe that for every problem there is a solution and for every challenging situation there is a right way to address it. In fact, in the authors' experience the really tough problems and situations never yield to easy answers, and there are often several answers: some more right, some less right, and none obvious or easy.

You should also realize and accept the fact that you can make the decision you feel is absolutely right and reflects your best self, but then discover that it turns out wrong. Daniel Thomas (page 121) found himself in that position. Your only consolation is that you followed your heart, you did what you knew to be right, and you were true to your values. And that sometimes has to be the only reward you get.

There's no doubt that, if you are already in a leadership position or hope someday to be, you will face situations that challenge your integrity right down to the core. We sincerely hope that, when those times come, this book will have proven to be an invaluable resource and a friend in need.